LOST
NEW LONDON

BILL MORSE

THE History PRESS

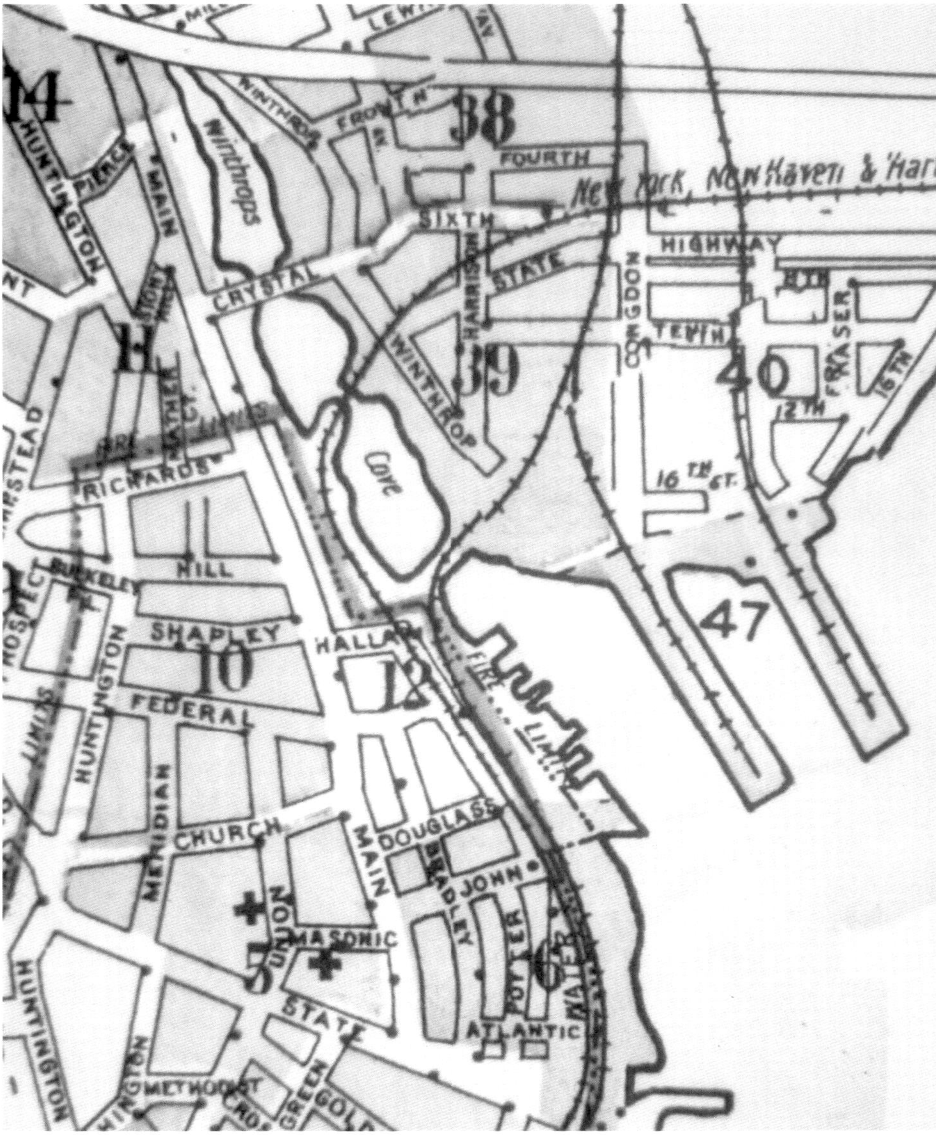

Sanborn Fire Insurance map of New London, 1954. *Library of Congress (LOC).*

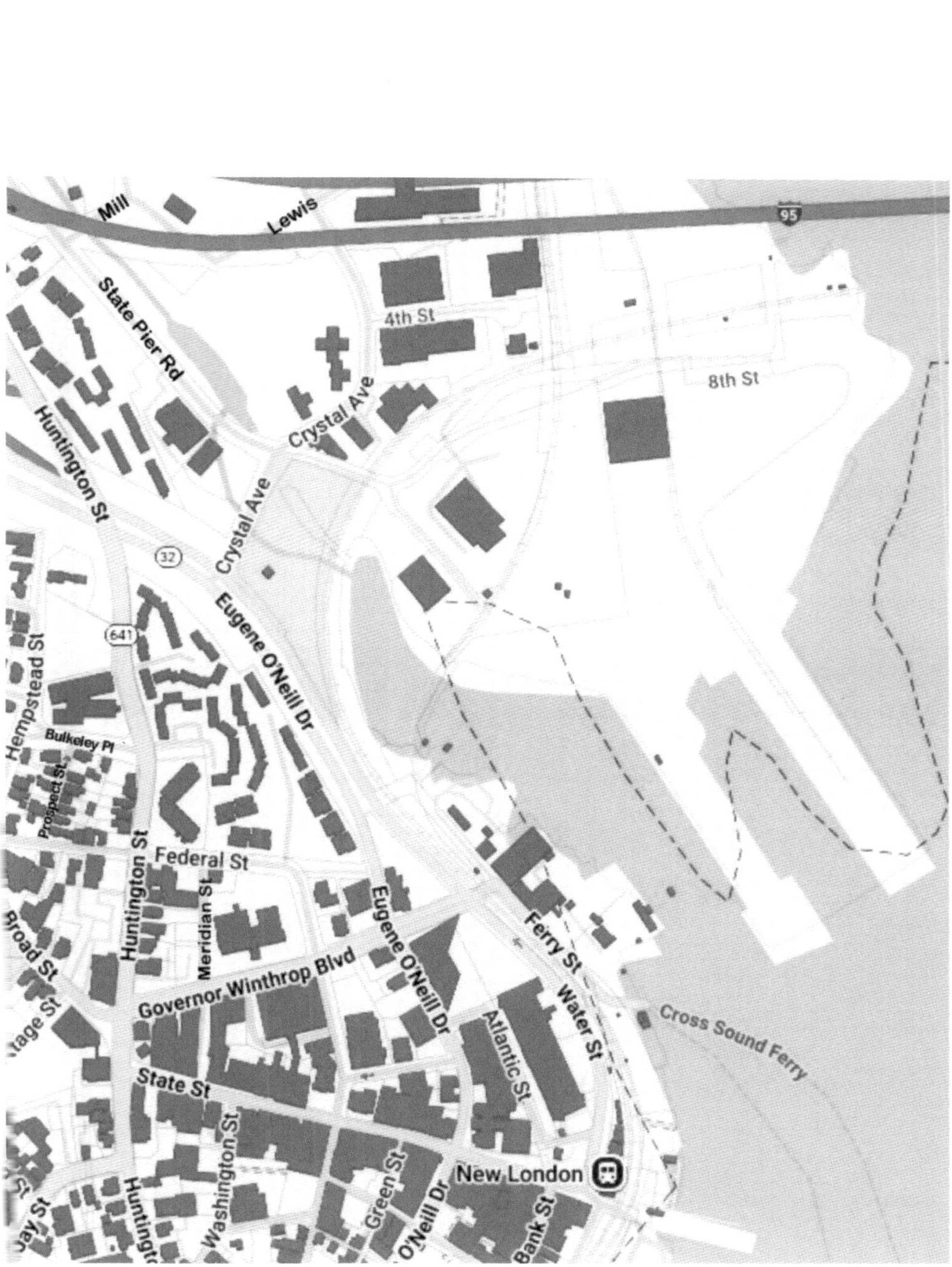

Main Street/Winthrop Cove area, 2025. *City of New London (CONL).*

Published by The History Press
An imprint of Arcadia Publishing
Charleston, SC
www.historypress.com

First published 2025

Manufactured in the United States

ISBN 9781467158954

Library of Congress Control Number: 2025941470

This collection of photographs and memories is dedicated to a pair of individuals who helped me appreciate the muse all of us hold within.

Mr. Art Lamoureux was a life coach, in the classroom and on the field.
His commanding presence pushed me into reading short stories, which I later attempted to write. Think of a gentle bear with wit and a sense of humor.
It was truly a blessing that he walked the hallways of St. Bernard High School in Montville, Connecticut.
Thank you, Mr. Lamoureux.

Mr. Mark Mirsky came to me decades later at City College in upper Manhattan.
The author of The Red Adam and other works, this Harpo Marx lookalike with a vending machine honey bun in his mouth listened intently to hundreds of readings, hundreds of pages of dreck, monotony and talent. He was our cheerleader from Canal Street, holding court in a watering hole on Hudson Street, intentionally on the iciest of nights when we would not wander.
Thank you, Mark.

CONTENTS

FOREWORD

For decades, as our society has continued to change, older communities like New London have faced repeated challenges in making this city's unique sense of place relevant to new generations of Americans. New Londoners (or Whalers) have seen their small port city experience a managed decline as housing, retail space and industry were often built elsewhere.

That has changed.

The downward spiral is reversing as more and more people seek out a secure and conveniently walkable urban environment with all the family-friendly amenities. In many ways, the better planning, marketing, communication, schools and funding are bringing back the lifestyles described in this book.

Michael E. Passero
Mayor, City of New London

The author (*left*) with Mayor Michael Passero, a friend since second grade, relaxing on the deck behind Muddy Waters Cafe, summer 2023.

ACKNOWLEDGEMENTS

The book you are holding in your hands would not have been possible without the imagery and assistance provided by the following people.

Bess Oldershaw gave me a shopping bag of color slides taken by her brother, George, while I was working on the first floor of 94 Golden Street in the early 2000s.

Laura Natusch and Alicia Primer of New London Landmarks gave me full access to their files, helping me fill out the missing Oldershaw slides and filling in more gaps by sharing with me appraisal forms and pictures used by the Redevelopment Agency. Tom Crouser provided me with helpful research advice, as did Mary Baker.

Steve Manuel and Pat Schaefer of the New London County Historical Society provided additional imagery and historical background.

Brian Sear, himself a historian with roots in Canterbury, scanned for me many site photos from a City of New London collection he and others had rescued from the basement of the Stanton Building. Mayor Michael Passero, city planner Felix Reyes, assistant building official Jamie Salmon, city clerk Jonathan Ayala and NLPD Chief Brian Wright were also most helpful with their assistance.

Tim Dwyer, publisher of *The Day*, graciously gave permission for the use of his company's photographs in this book. The reflections in *Day* articles by Margaret Stacy, John Foley, Ann Baldelli and Carol Kimball proved invaluable in their coverage of the Main Street area streetscapes and those who lived and worked in them.

Raven and Angela of the New London Public Library reference desk helped me with imagery scanning from the holdings in the library's local history room.

Tom Schuch, New London historian, provided me access to a wealth of narrative involving the early slave and freeman experiences in New London.

Benjamin Panciera and Andrew Lopez of the Connecticut College Library provided me with period *Conscience* newsletters from the New London branch of the NAACP.

Brian Rogers of the McGuire Maritime Library at the Customs House gave me access to the Savannah imagery.

Carla Lesh of the Hudson Maritime Society gave me access to the group's maritime salvage holdings.

Jim Streeter of the Groton Historical Society provided me with info and imagery focusing on the Mohican ferry and Groton Landing.

Jean Jordan, Val Tamano, Leila Shakkour, Nicole Thomas, Chuck Potter, Elaine Maynard Adams, Bebe Norman, Manny Rivera, Reid Burdick, Gerard Massad, Shirley Beckwith and Rayna Duggan Danik shared with me family pictures and histories.

Elaine Maynard Adams and Bob Ferrara shared images and the history of the JayPro sports equipment company, now in Waterford.

In closing, let me thank Mike DiMauro, Greg Stone, Fuji Fulgueras, Joe Dimaggio, Lou Pica, Joel Riley, Peg Curtin, Vinnie Scarano, Peter Detmold, Larry and Catherine Keating, John Ruddy, Barbara Timken and Harrison Shoesmith.

And thank you, dear reader, for your interest in New London.

INTRODUCTION

Welcome, dear reader!

Let me begin by taking a quote from Jane Jacobs in her book *The Death and Life of Great American Cities.* Here she quotes a tenant in East Harlem airing a shared anger against a large rectangular lawn within the housing project:

> *Nobody cared what we wanted when they built this place. They threw our houses down and pushed us here and pushed our friends somewhere else. We don't have a place around here to get a cup of coffee or a newspaper even, or borrow fifty cents. Nobody cared about what we needed. But the big men come and look at the grass and say, "Isn't it wonderful! Now the poor have everything!"*

East Harlem, 1961. As we continue through this collection of memories and photographs, we will come to realize that these wonderful observations would be echoed in New London and hundreds of other cities, large and small, across our country. In the end, we'll have a much clearer idea of what worked and what didn't and why that all-important sense of place is missing in many of our urban communities.

Chapter 1

THE PARADE

Today is June 17, 2024. We are on the Parade, considered by many to be the heart of New London. If we look east toward the river, we see what has been described as an ark-like structure from another century: Union Station.

Initially used by the New London Northern (later the Central Vermont) and the New York, New Haven and Hartford (or, simply, the New Haven), this 1887 Richardson ark of transportation suffered from the neglect of the New Haven and later Penn Central bankruptcies. Ironically, the last profits from the road came from the transport of raw materials needed for construction of the Connecticut Turnpike, later a part of I-95, in the late 1950s to early '60s.

The unseen benefit is that through this lack of cash, the New Haven never had the money to relocate and build a new Union Station, significantly downsizing its capacity and permanence to that of a plexiglass aluminum-framed bus shelter. In the local press, *The Day* paper published the article "Union Station's Days Numbered" on January 14, 1965, citing in the last paragraph that "few will mourn Union Station's demise. It is an ugly, dirty architectural monstrosity." Many New Londoners and visitors concurred. After riding three trains from San Francisco in '47, my father got off in New London on his way to the Coast Guard Academy. After years of heavy wartime passenger traffic, the station was exhausted—cracked, peeling walls; battered floors and doors; missing lights; dirty, broken windows; loose bricks and roof slate waiting for the next storm. It was not a welcoming first impression.

Above: Union Station. *Author.*

Left: Claire Dale. *Courtesy George Oldershaw.*

Had it not been for Claire Dale, a forty-four-year-old concert pianist who came to New London via Connecticut College, Union Station would be on the front cover of this "Lost" book. Along with her team of volunteers, she was successful in stoking much-needed preservation efforts in New London. Indeed, after the loss of New York's Pennsylvania Station and New London's Neptune Building, the attitude toward art and function was changing. As the Winthrop Cove redevelopment project was in its final phase, the agency decided in 1971 that it was purchasing the 1887 Henry Hobson Richardson railroad station with the intention of demolishing it for a smaller transportation center. It was blocking the view of the river, civic leaders said. Interestingly enough, in 1965, as most of the buildings along the east side of Main Street had disappeared, people remarked with glee that now it was possible to see the Gold Star Bridge while walking toward Hodges Square—not the Eiffel Tower, but the Gold Star Bridge.

After five years in which a developer and financing came together in 1976, the designated national landmark was finally out of danger. Supporters like Claire Dale and architect George Notter proved that preservation and economically sound repurposing could work.

Today, many older communities benefit from the charm and architectural beauty of the past and have local organizations dedicated to keeping this vision of their hometowns alive. New London Landmarks is one such group, founded through the efforts of Claire Dale. Today, Alicia Primer is the group's director. As a high school student in the mid-'70s, she worked with Claire in raising support and awareness for Union Station. If you wish to see more of the Union Station story, New London Landmarks has posted the thirty-minute video "The Rescue of Mr. Richardson's Last Station 1978" on YouTube.

George Oldershaw was another proponent for preservation. Most of the pictures providing the backbone of this book came from his collection. George lived up the hill on Amity Street and worked at Pfizer in Groton. In the photo seen here, he is standing by a cut of tanker cars stretching into the Hess fuel tank yard just north of Charles Pfizer & Co. In '73, George had a Greek Revival home moved when St. Sophia Church bought the property with plans to demolish it. He and his sister Bess took this orphan and created the Vaux Hall, an elegant restaurant and gathering place during the '70s and '80s. George passed in 1990, having created a rare and valuable legacy for the New London community. Some twenty years ago, Bess gave me a bag of slides taken by George, mostly during his pre-redevelopment street wanderings in 1961. Hence, my interest in New London's rich past came alive.

George Oldershaw. *Courtesy Bess Oldershaw.*

The whale's tail. *Author.*

It seems only fitting that New London should have a whale's tail fountain flush with the pavement as if it were the sea. Much of New London's earlier wealth came from the whaling industry, which gave light in dark spaces. The fountain speaks of water, man against the leviathan, adventure, hardship, sacrifice, cruelty, faith and hope. Much of what was built in that era from the 1820s to the 1850s now lives on only through the streets we are about to explore. My hope, dear reader, is that you enjoy this nickel tour.

The City of New London from 1964 to '65 took survey pictures of various properties within the Winthrop Cove Urban Renewal Area. Thanks to Brian Sear, public works director, this collection has been placed at my disposal. The photograph seen here is the first in that group. Today, in 2024, we have the whale's tail fountain. In 1965 stood the bus terminal, a luncheonette, rented rooms and a restaurant at approximately this same location.

The New London bus terminal at 15 State Street is owned by Moses Savin, who also owns the local bus company, the New Haven and Shoreline Railway. When I was a child, we rode his buses to school, and after someone

The bus terminal building. *CONL.*

stuck a tennis ball in the muffler, he boarded the bus and paid us a brief visit. Mr. Savin was also, at one time, the mayor, a city councilor and a past president of the B.P. Learned House, then at 230 Main Street.

Leo Mantzaris and his wife, Thoila, of Groton, ran the lunch counter off the waiting room of the bus terminal, where customers enjoyed strong coffee and no-nonsense service in the late evening hours. The drama lit by a single working phone booth sometimes spilled over to the counter. An officer or other able-bodied man was usually nearby. With the station house around the corner and interactions plentiful, foot patrols were the norm.

A BRIEF VISIT

> *At 2:30 this morning three officers of the NLPD took in Gloria W., 19, and Katie K., 22, both of New York City under suspicion of night walking. According to the report the young ladies were without funds and in the company of several Submarine Base sailors. Brought before Judge S. in police court, both women were released under suspension of judgment and instructed to leave town immediately.*
>
> —The Day, *September 25, 1942*

The terminal building, itself a holdover from the late whaling era, came down in '67. Judging from the debris pile, a clawfoot tub and sink on each of the above floors provided the long-vanished business travelers, peddlers, wayward husbands, sailors on leave (or not) and fugitives an opportunity to freshen up. Most had not the cash to go farther up State Street.

The terminal's neighbor to the right also offered quick and easy accommodation, as evidenced by the small "rooms" sign hanging stubbornly on the left-hand door at 5 State Street. Jim Louziotis owns the building and runs the place behind the double doors at 3 State, the Manhattan Restaurant. Lime-green tiles cover the first-floor façade, and an orange-red "Manhattan Restaurant" sign goes on in the plate-glass window when the restaurant is open. Albanian-born chef Stephen Krotsis, a member of St. Sophia Greek Orthodox Church, worked here until his death in 1954, according to *The Day* of May 27, 1954.

Today's expanded Parade also covers the site of the Neptune Building. In the image seen here, behind speaker Lonnie Braxton and other civic leaders gathered for Juneteenth stretches Atlantic Street behind The Day building

Site of the former Neptune building. *Author.*

and the former Savings Bank of New London. This straight run of Atlantic Street was the former North Bank Street, which started at State Street on the western side of the Neptune Building approximately where our speakers have gathered today.

The Parade has always been a visible piece of New London real estate. At the time of the British burning in 1781, there stood on this spot the first Episcopal church. During a Sunday service, Patriot congregants pulled from the pulpit the rector as he was about to offer the customary prayer for King George III. During that British walk-through led by General Arnold, the soldiers lit by torch any building thought to shelter enemies of the Crown or hold supplies or booty from the privateering (attacks on British ships). The fires destroyed that first church, the courthouse, the prison and the Parade fort.

Sometime in the late 1790s, while the "jockey trade" was still going strong—that is, brigs taking down to the West Indies horses, forage and hardware while bringing back rum and molasses (and, earlier on, slaves)—Charles Bolles had built a large warehouse-like structure he used for his grocery and liquor business. Much to the chagrin of wives, sweethearts and temperance advocates, a saloon known as "the hole in the wall" opened in the cellar and for a time, until the late 1840s, was the main watering hole in town. In time, however, as more and more households accepted rum as a diet staple, the novelty of the place ran its course. The property passed from a McClintock to a Lawrence to a Brandegee. When the photograph seen here was taken in the 1860s, the building was already being called the "old yellow store." Note the brick building to the right with the single window. Yes, the future bus terminal. In my opinion, that side wall facing the old yellow store was built as a firewall complete with parapet as protection from a spreading fire. In 1896, former Mayor Brandegee sold the yellow store property to the city in anticipation of a planned five-story brick "ornament," and in 1897, the city sold the old yellow store to a developer for $15,000, as noted in *The Day* on December 28, 1897.

The developer of the proposed ornament, the G.M. Long Co., ran a seafood market on the other side of the Parade on Railroad Avenue (South Water Street) and held a naming contest for what had initially been called the "Long Building." The winner was to collect a five-dollar prize. Six entries came in with the name "Neptune" and two others with the name

Old Yellow building. *New London Public Library (NLPL).*

"Poseidon." In the end, *The Day* reported on October 17, 1899, each of the six took home a dollar.

"Salt Water Notes" was a periodic column in *The Day* that covered "bits of life and color from New London wharves" around the turn of the century. Its "thumbnail" was a bearded, large-headed bald man, wizened by years on the water, who wrote with a quill in a ledger while smoking a pipe, his captain's hat long retired. On the topic of naming the new building, he simply wrote on October 25, 1899, "'Neptune building' sounds nice and salty."

"POSEIDON" OR "NEPTUNE"?

As you can see in this 1901 photograph, a seafood market never did make it into the Neptune Building, even though Southern New England Telephone did relocate its exchange to the top floor. The high-end men's clothing company E.D. Steele moved quickly into the store, but the luster of newness

Neptune building, circa 1901. *NLPL.*

Neptune building, circa 1961. *George Oldershaw.*

began to fade. During both world wars, soldiers and sailors were billeted on the upper floors, with foreseeably mixed results. In 1951, a display ad appeared in *The Day* offering "office space" for lease on the upper floors. The Neptune Hotel was waiting for another war.

In 1961, the street level was still alive with full commercial occupancy. Many remember the Army Navy Store anchoring one half of the space since the late '40s at 37, the Paramount Restaurant at 27, the Elite Barber Shop at 25 and Ann's Coffee Shop at 23.

Chapter 2

ATLANTIC STREET

NEWSFLASH

Phillip Bruno and Morris Rice, both barbers, smell gas upon entering their home at 9 North Bank Street after an evening at Ocean Beach. In the basement, they discover a loose fitting in the gas line that they immediately tighten. The smell persists. Above them at 5 North Bank Street is the Konstantine and Mallach Restaurant, where staff is cleaning up. They report the gas smell to Connecticut Power, which dispatches an employee. Back in the basement, the two barbers notice the meter hands moving quickly on the gas line leading into the Handy Lunch on Atlantic just around the corner.

The Connecticut Power employee now arrived, the three men break through the front door of the luncheonette and are hit by the gas. The heater valve behind the counter is full open. Also behind the counter is Charles Baldwin, in his Sunday best, lying on pages from *The Day* newspaper covering the linoleum floor. The men drag the luncheonette owner outside onto the sidewalk. Dr. Satti arrives to treat the inert Baldwin. The ambulance arrives, and the man is rushed to the hospital and placed on a pulmotor. Baldwin survives, and Lawrence and Memorial (L&M) releases him a month later.

So why the suicide attempt with "illuminating gases"?

Charles Baldwin had made a fair amount of money from the Handy Lunch, enough in fact to sink eight grand into a larger restaurant across the Parade at 5 Railroad Avenue (South Water Street). Trouble brewed as

Atlantic Street. *George Oldershaw.*

the new restaurant was slow in covering expenses. According to *The Day* of July 22, 1926, Baldwin grew despondent and eventually turned to suicide.

A little more than a decade and another world war passed while Lauriano Navarro worked in other restaurants. In 1950, the luncheonette spot on Atlantic was open after the departure of Stephen Pappas. The following year, Lou's Lunch opened, remaining in business until redevelopment shut it down for good with a wrecking crane in early '67.

Atlantic Street ran behind the Neptune Building from Water to Potter Street at the east end of the Neptune to North Bank Street at the west end of the Neptune. Before the British burned the block, it was called Prison Street. For a while it was a busy stretch, but by 1961, there were but three locations remaining: the Wonder Bar restaurant at 17; a municipal pumping station; and Lou's Lunch, run by Navarro, at 33.

Chapter 3

NORTH BANK (BRADLEY) STREET

La vida es un carnaval.
—Celia Cruz, Cuban singer, songwriter

We are behind the Neptune Building at the beginning of North Bank, or Bradley Street, as it was known before 1922. The east side of the G.M. Williams Company is behind us. That store carried almost anything you could walk or ride away with—athletic gear, housewares, tools, paints, bicycles, tricycles, you name it. The main entrance is around the corner on the Parade. In front of us at 5 North Bank was the Konstantine and Mallach Restaurant during Prohibition (1920–33) and, when the beer was flowing afterward, a series of package stores running up to the late '50s, when William Sanders of Norwich opened Sander's Pet Shop. Sanders offered puppies bedded in the window, parakeets in silver-domed cages, tropical fish in a large aquarium, white mice and foraging hamsters, turtles in a personal plastic pool with a plastic palm tree and all the foods, medicines and yummies to ensure these future pets a long and happy life. Local Brownie and Girl Scout troops would visit Sanders's shop as part of their animal care badge, according to *The Day* of May 1, 1958.

By 1965, the fish, birds and people had been gone for over four years, and with redevelopment on the horizon, this property, like so many others, would sit vacant, a tempting target for vandals, scrappers, arsonists and the homeless.

Above: 5 North Bank Street, 1964. *CONL.*

Opposite: 13–15 North Bank, 1961. *New London Landmarks (NLL).*

This 1961 view of 13 (store) and 15 (two apartments above) North Bank Street was taken as part of redevelopment's appraisal process. For a year or so, the Polaris Action Group, also known as the Committee for Non-Violence (CFNV), used the storefront as a field activity office seeking to curtail the construction of atomic submarines such as the Nautilus (571). Neither the sailors from the sub base nor the workers at Electric Boat appreciated their efforts. On at least one occasion reported in a group newsletter, sailors from the base in Groton entered the storefront quite ready to vent their anger. Fortunately, cooler heads prevailed, and violence was averted. The sub base commanding officer soon after ordered that stretch of North Bank Street off-limits to all service personnel, reported *The Day* on August 17, 1960. In the image seen here, note the hanging sign and the peace symbol painted on a sheet of plywood covering the left plate-glass window. On the right is 9, Wolf's Barber Shop. For many years, as was the custom, the Wolf family lived upstairs at 11. Mr. Wolf took in boarding barbers who worked with him below in the shop, barbers like Phillip Bruno and Morris Rice. On the left at 19 was the Liberty Restaurant, with apartments above at 21. A narrow walkway between the buildings led to a brick addition, 17, which offered further accommodation. Anthony Cosantino, a World War II U.S. Navy vet and chef, managed the Liberty for many years after buying it in 1947. He also owned and managed the Thames Diner at 35 Crystal Avenue, another business to be removed through redevelopment.

Let's go back to 13–15 North Bank Street for a moment. Look closely at the center window over the shop entrance. I believe we are looking at Isabelle Jones gazing out at the photographer. The year before, in '64, she fell asleep while meat cooked on the stove. Fortunately, a friend was coming to check on her and the neighbor above. The friend saw smoke coming out of the open window, ran and pulled an alarm up the street.

With the help of the neighbor, the two pulled Jones from her apartment. An ambulance brought her to the hospital, where she was treated for smoke inhalation. She survived to pose for this last picture in her home a year later. The fire department cleared out the smoke with an air circulator. Damage was minimal. Union Realty, a part of the Beit Bros. supermarket chain, owned and managed the property.

13–15 North Bank, 1964. *CONL.*

We are on the western side of the street now, at the truck loading entrance on the left and the southeast corner of The Day newspaper plant on the right. Note and remember that marker at the brick corner. This mundane location has many stories.

Dart Hall marker. *Author.*

The loading dock location in 1961 was a three-story frame apartment building with storefronts. The cornice had detailed bracket and dental work similar to that of the Williams Bakery building at Green and Golden Streets, built in 1882.

The storefronts at 28–30 North Bank served the Visual Arts sign company of Joan Russell and William H. Babcock, both of Groton. Their trade was neon and plastic signs along with silk screen printing, sign maintenance and placement. Since '54, their firm had taken on the Christmas decorations downtown. Over seventy local businesses collaborated at the time, reported *The Day* of December 13, 1960.

Threatened with redevelopment, Visual Arts bought the ruined New London Brewery site under the bridge at the corner of Mill and Winthrop Streets from the Max Rogovin Estate ("rovin' with Rogovin"), only to be further impacted by plans for a second bridge over the Thames, reported *The Day* on May 20, 1960.

Above: New addition to The Day building, 1961. *George Oldershaw.*

Left: USS *Tringa* sub salvage vessel. *LOC.*

In one of the five apartments above lived a sailor, Robert C. Tandy, twenty-one, the last resident before redevelopment took down the building in '66. When he wasn't out on the road improving his small truck driving skills, as reported in *The Day*, shipmate Tandy served aboard the sub vessel *Tringa*.

On April 11, 1963, the U.S. Navy declared the atomic submarine *Thresher*, SSN 593, "lost" during deep dive trials some two hundred miles east of Boston. Counting the crew and support staff from Electric Boat, 129 souls rested on the bottom, like so many sailors before them. This was, however, the single largest loss of life. The *Tringa* was part of the recovery effort, noted *The Day* on April 11.

In 1961, The Day building's expansion was a year old. What was there before? It was a frame house with two storefronts at 34–38 and a three-story commercial brick building at 42–46 with apartments and a third-floor meeting hall. Hiram Marcus had opened his men's outfitting store around 1917 and sold the business and buildings to the Wilensky family in the late '20s.

Mrs. Wilensky owned the frame house. Over the decades, a Chinese (Mon Frond) and a Jewish restaurant did business on the second floor. The Nadeau family settled in later during the '50s. The last tenant at 36 was Homer Davis (who would marry Margaret Stokes from 42 Potter Street). He ran a tool sharpening, rental and servicing business. His neighbor in 38 was Arthur H. McDonald, an army veteran of both world wars and a retired maintenance man from Seaside in Waterford. His trade was antiques.

Mr. Wilensky owned and managed Marcus jeans, the local representative for Lee's boots and men's outerwear. From the mid-'20s to the early '40s, the meeting hall space was the men's lodge under the guidance of Richard Mansfield, superintendent of the Learned House. Per their ability, men put in a couple of hours work cleaning basements and yards, whitewashing and cutting and bundling kindling wood in exchange for a hot meal (such as

Hiram Marcus & Company, 1959. *From* The Day.

hamburg steak, potato, bread and coffee), a shower, clean clothes and one of thirty cots. Tom Cornell (not to be confused with the radio man Tom Cornell, who put "pep in your set" across the street at 43) would sign men in seven nights a week as a sort of nightclub bouncer. Every now and then, he'd call in the police from diagonally across the street to do what his crippled legs couldn't: break up a fight, toss out a drunk or two, wrestle a hidden flask away. The intoxicated would-be lodger would wake up in police court before a judge admonishing him for ingratitude. Five dollars or five days. Next case!

When lack of funding threatened to close the men's lodge, the outbreak of war kept the shelter open and Tom Cornell busy as newly arrived defense plant workers had jobs, but no place to stay. The empty rooms and cold-water flats around North Bank and Main Streets filled up.

The First World War was equally demanding of space. Known then as Liberty Hall, the third-floor space went to the War Camp Club, a sort of USO where soldiers and sailors could find relaxation, entertainment and sometimes future wives. Elizabeth Jeter of 113 Green Street often organized the concerts, movies, dances, talks and other welcoming events that broke up the loneliness and boredom of the soldiers and sailors. As the armed forces were segregated, so were the War Camp Clubs; the Black club stayed at Liberty Hall, and the white club was in the Harris Building at a higher-rent State Street address. On November 18, 1919, Liberty Hall offered a vaudeville-type show and a New York jazz band to a mixed audience without incident.

The race riots of the summer before—of the white sailor against Black sailor, the Black sailor against white sailor—had been an ugly reminder of the underlying blind hatred arriving by train, bus, boat or simply simmering at home. Earlier that spring on one occasion in April and another in May—as reported in *The Day* on April 16, 1919, and May 28, 1919—a retired congressman from South Carolina, George Washington Murray, born of enslaved parents, self-taught and later a teacher, came to the hall and spoke of self-reliance, honesty and the dignity of self-determination. Nearly two hundred sailors, soldiers and civilians listened without disturbance and without harassment thereafter.

South Carolina Congressman Washington Murray. *LOC.*

The story on 42 North Bank Street goes back even further. In an 1876 "picture map," the building's address was different. People were calling the street Bradley after an early settler. There as the frame house with two storefronts (now 12) and the three-story brick building with a meeting space called Dart Hall, named for the owner, builder Leonard Dart, who in the 1840s was just getting into what would become a lucrative gas lighting and heating business. On the weekend of May 13, 1848, Frederick Douglass gave four talks on the abolition of slavery to a receptive audience.

It is important to remember that during colonial times, New London as a seaport conducted trade with the West Indies or Caribbean. Horses and forged goods went south on ships that brought back rum, sugar and West African slaves. Connecticut was the last of the New England states to abolish slavery in 1848, just months after Frederick Douglass's visit to Dart Hall. Over the decades, local families enriched themselves with the trade. The New London census of 1810 counted 147 free colored people and 13 slaves within the population. By 1820, that number was 168 free and 6 enslaved, according to Caulkins's *History of New London*.

After Dart Hall, the next building at 20 Bradley is the Mission or Bradley Chapel. Second Congregational Church funds built this chapel in 1867 under the direction of pastor Reverend B.G. Wilcox. In 1859, he started with a class of seven children who were "miserable, wretched and ragged." The programs soon offered food, clothing, music, storytelling and manual arts in a spiritually uplifting environment. Summer school began in 1862 with a balance of recreation and academic instruction. Volunteers also engaged in outreach through home visits.

After the turn of the century, Billings P. Learned, a wealthy and generous Wall Street broker living in the Pequot Colony of New London, worked with Superintendent Richard Mansfield in gaining the support and involvement of the banks, the hospital, the YMCA, Connecticut College, the schools and the police in reaching mission goals. In 1916, Learned passed away, leaving much of his estate to the mission. A year later, in recognition of this generosity, the board of directors voted to change the name of the chapel to the B.P. Learned House.

If you walk north along what is now Atlantic Street past the 1960 addition to The Day building, you'll notice an even older addition to the newspaper. This is where the chapel and another building stood. In 1925, *The Day* bought the chapel and adjoining property for this earlier expansion. With proceeds from the sale, the Learned House was able to set up men's lodging in the former Liberty (née Dart) Hall third floor and secure the former 1850

Lawrence villa at 230 Main Street for children's programming, wrote Dave Carlson in *The Day* on April 14, 1959.

Before crossing the street to the police station, a word about Bradley Street would be helpful.

In a *New London Day* column from "the Tattler" on March 11, 1913, the anonymous writer takes the reader on a Sunday stroll along Bradley Street. His enthusiasm for the street is apparent in that he prefers the street's variety, heterogeneousness, unexpectedness and "numerical bulk" against any other earthly legal thoroughfare. In his view, street cleaning is counterproductive in that he senses a certain pride in "frowsiness" and coarseness. By embarking on what may be "the dirtiest street in the world," the article cites a "triumphant distinction in the degree of our disgrace."

During this walk, the Tattler observes the following:

- the ruin of an umbrella
- an ancient tea caddy minus the bottom
- all manner of food cans
- a "spiritually gone" cat, but very much present in body
- waste paper, the amount of which is hard to fathom
- flower sacks
- cereal packages
- a child's dress
- two hats
- four odd shoes
- bottles
- tons of mud mixed with a granulated sum of a thousand sources
- half a corset
- ashes
- three beer kegs
- "and everything under the light of heaven, but money."

"How can so few people keep the street so marvelously littered?" the writer asks while noting the stiff competition from John, Potter and Douglass Streets.

A day later in a letter to the editor, Bradley Mission Superintendent Mansfield notes the mostly futile attempts at sustaining under his direction a juvenile street-cleaning league and wonders if a sidewalk on his side of the street might not "help the sinner reach the mission doors."

Also at about this time, April 5, 1912, an article titled "Keepers of the Dives" came out in *The Day*, reporting on the results of a recent raid on "houses of ill-fame in the Tenderloin." Twenty-eight women in smart, expensive dress appeared before the judge in police court on charges of

NEW LONDON, C
1876
BROWN COTTON GIN MANUFACTORY

Picture map, 1876. *LOC.*

conducting and frequenting houses of prostitution. Looking more like a Fifth Avenue fashion show on Easter, according to the reporter, the ladies drew in a capacity crowd of onlookers, with many turned away. Pooling their resources, the women all made bond. The prosecuting attorney named nine of the twenty-eight women proprietors. Four of the nine had set up shop on Bradley:

- Queenie LaFrance, 41 Bradley Street
- Mary Fitch, 9 Bradley Street
- Frances Adams, 45 Bradley Street
- Dolly Snow, 33 Bradley Street

The other five ladies represented Atlantic and Potter Streets. Each of the nine charged proprietors was given a $100 fine and orders to desist. The judge did not charge the remaining defendants, or "frequenters," based on the understanding that they would leave town within thirty-six hours.

The setup for each dive depended on cash-hungry landlords willing to rent out their vacant storefronts at twice the market rate with no questions asked and on a weekly basis. Number 9 Bradley Street, later a legitimate barbershop (Wolf's), had candy samples in the window along with nonalcoholic beverages that were often spiked. A head-high curtain hung behind this display, making a look-through nearly impossible. There was no sign. At night, a soft light illuminated the window—a red glow, I'd imagine.

In 1916, the city council and mayor set up a police committee to deal with the practice of vice on Bradley Street. The writer in "Timely Views by the Commentator" on August 21, 1916, compared this committee with the Pickwick Club immortalized by Charles Dickens in that he saw a very long learning curve ahead for the appointed group. Unlike the Tattler from three years earlier, the Commentator took a different view of the sanitary conditions present on the street: "Bradley Street is a name for a New London condition which has been a stench in the nostrils of citizens for many, many months. It is high time the authorities discovered it."

The writer went on to mention a particular landlord owning houses on Bradley Street and renting them out to outsiders who had become, by way of intentionally blocking the sidewalk and making sleep impossible, inconsiderate neighbors. In short order, the police committee called for a public hearing in which the mayor, police chief and three aldermen (city councilors) attended along with thirty Bradley Street residents and homeowners. After the hearing, the police chief met with the landlord, who, unaware that the basement of his house at 107 Bradley had been illegally sublet (this remains an issue today), offered his full cooperation and had the sheriff serve the four adults with papers of eviction. The people left, and so did the crowd jostling into the gutter and intrusive nocturnal noise on warm summer nights, reported *The Day* on August 23.

In 1922, the New London City Council had given Bradley Street a new, orderly name: North Bank Street. Congress had already passed the Volstead Act, which prohibited the preparation and sale of drinks with more than 0.5 percent alcohol. Raids by federal agents aided by local police were sporadic but did take place. Sometimes the captain in charge simply posted one of his men in uniform outside a known "joint" location, as happened at the southeast corner of North Bank and John Streets.

The name "saloon" disappeared from business listings. Former saloonkeepers were now simply in the "beverage" trade. The red-light image of New London vice so well portrayed in the work of playwright Eugene O'Neill and other writers was to become a thing of the past—that is, if civic leaders had anything to do with it.

The taste for gambling, prostitution and drink did not go away, and the three were often available in a single location known as a joint, dive or "resort," most within walking distance of one another—no DUIs!

In the November 25, 1922 edition of the *New London Evening Day*, a certain Uncle Jonah came up with mental examination questions for police applicants, published on page 8 under the heading "Ambergris":

1. Spell "supernumerary" and get it right the first time.
2. Where would you prefer to be doing duty—at Riverside Park in December or at the Capitol Theatre?
3. Is the police station located on North Bank Street?
4. Name the clubs in the city where there is no gambling.
5. What route would you take in going from the Neptune Building to the Parade?
6. Have you any scruples against carrying a white night stick?
7. Have you any tattoo marks or moles which would serve to identify you if you happened to become lost or never found?
8. Have you cirrhosis of the liver, flat feet, or ingrowing toenails which would prevent you from marching in a parade?
9. Have you any friends? If not, is that the reason why you seek a position on the force?

Police headquarters at 57 North Bank Street was a relatively new facility that replaced an antiquated and inadequate one on Potter Street. The value of a better funded, organized and educated public force was starting to become apparent to New London's civic leaders, and so a handsome brick

New London police headquarters, circa 1920. *NLPL.*

station was erected with a walk-in entrance on North Bank Street and a police wagon entrance on Potter.

The Day bought headquarters in '46 after the department moved to the former Stanton school at 111 Union Street and attempted to rent out the building for office use. These events followed an unsuccessful bid by the city to buy the Brainard & Armstrong silk mill at auction, demolish it and erect a modern municipal multidepartmental building with parking. The Sanborn Fire Insurance map for '54 shows a "state training facility" for the former police building, but my limited research found nothing more.

On the right side is a laundry sign for 53, the Sam Wing Sing laundry, with two apartments above at 55. Known as "Sam" (his American name was solely for business purposes), this young Chinese entrepreneur had an able mentor, Mr. Hong Wah, New London's first Chinese laundry operator, in 1880. Suffering from depression and worsening health, "Hong" threw himself in the water that following summer by Coit's wharf. His body remained under water for over a week and finally surfaced with a "jump," showing hands clasped as if in prayer. During the burial ceremony, beer, not tea, was poured atop Hong's resting place should he grow thirsty in this final journey to "the flowery kingdom." Five years later, Hong Wah's bones were exhumed, cleaned and sent to his homeland in China.

During this time, Sam remained operating Hong's laundry business at 3 Bradley Street (Wolf's Barber Shop) while also operating another laundry at 25 Green Street with partner Ching Wing Sing. Together, they ran this laundry from 1886 to 1900.

And not without some drama: on August 14, 1896, news of the presumed murder of Mary Burke in her Green Street apartment above (center door) made the front page of *The Day*. Details on the condition of the body and the presence of an iron on the floor next to Burke's injured head fueled much tongue wagging. The coroner came down from Norwich and ruled "death by natural causes" the following day.

On a more festive note, Sam helped celebrate July 4 by entertaining passersby with an evening fireworks display at the corner of Green and State

Sam Woo laundry, 1961. *George Oldershaw.*

Streets. Such displays were common on the vacant lots and aboard some of the yachts at anchor in the harbor. *The Day* of July 5, 1896, reported a large turnout.

In 1894, Sam moved his Bradley Street laundry up the street next to the future police station. A few things happened there of note, and *The Day* was there to report them.

In 1892, Congress passed an act whereby all Chinese citizens had to register their name and address and have their photographs taken. On August 24, the newspaper dispatched a reporter to go from laundry to laundry to report on the local Chinese reaction.

"Price of picture? How often in newspaper?"

"When you have other names, you come back for mine."

"I know nothing."

"Okay with me."

"Laundry ready Saturday night."

While managing up to three laundries, Sam also had time to help out at the Mon Frond restaurant at 12 Bradley Street. Through a series of reports, *The Day* kept readers on top of the "Chop suey wrangle." On February 13, 1902, four intoxicated men entered the restaurant and ordered chop suey. On a previous visit, one of the men had given Sam trouble with payment, so Sam wanted payment in advance. The men squabbled over the price, as they were charged a dollar when the going rate for four orders was fifteen cents apiece. One fell back into a chair and was unable to eat. Another started tossing teacups around the restaurant.

Sam hit the teacup tosser on the head and then disappeared into the back to inform the owner. A short time later, a policeman found William Crandall bleeding from a head wound on Douglass Street. The injured man pressed charges against Sam, and New London's best-known "Celestial" was brought into police court for breach of peace.

So, what is a "Celestial"? The emperor of China was known as "the son of heaven." By extension, those living within his celestial empire were known as "Celestials."

A week and a half went by. The judge nolled the assault charge against Sam when one of the four went missing, and the prosecution's case fell apart.

The Day reported in June 1901 that the police acted on a tip and raided the Mon Frond restaurant, charging past Sam and up the stairs to the apartment above. They discovered a group of men seated around a table playing "fan tan," a Chinese game of chance played with buttons or cards. Money was on the table. Police arrested ten Celestials, charging them with gambling. Most likely, each payed a five-dollar fine in police court. Though he'd yelled a warning in Mandarin to the men above, the court left Sam alone, as he was neither the owner nor could any connection be proven between him and the fan tan players.

Years later, three Internal Revenue agents accompanied by a member of the local police raided Chinese laundries in the city looking for evidence of the opium trade. The agents found none at 53 Bradley Street, reported *The Day* on January 15, 1920.

A brief mention should be made of the colonial-era home to the left of police headquarters, 73, with the eight-pane-over-twelve window. It belonged to former mayor Brian F. Mahan and was run as a furnished rooms house administered by Mrs. J.F. Choyniski. Evidently a stickler on accounts, Choyniski once enlisted the help of a policeman in detraining a former boarder headed out of town while owing the house $5.35, reported *The Day* on July 11, 14.

In the early morning hours of January 17, 1917, a match fire vacated "The Home," and so it remained, seemingly forgotten, until a newly formed building committee with some of the former mayor's best political friends decided to act. After Mahan missed a scheduled appearance before the group, an order for the demolition of The Home quickly went out.

The subsequent back and forth between the committee and Mahan made the press (*The Day* of August 10, 1918), and while there was little doubt the house could be repaired, the prevailing sentiment was that the former mayor had shirked his civic duty and so The Home must come down. A sheriff's order for demolition sealed the building's fate.

Continuing down the east side of North Bank Street, we're pausing at the W.R. Perry building, erected in 1899. Perry was in real estate (he bought and subdivided a farm offering great views on New London's Town Hill) and was in the wholesale ice business, harvesting from Cohanzie and Waterford ponds in January. Much like the men picked to help unload cargo from ships at the State Pier, the foreman picked men who showed up at the pond early on cold mornings when it looked like the pond would remain frozen for at least a couple of days. First picks went to men with families and the unemployed.

Samuel Levin owned and managed a saloon at 268 Main Street starting in 1912. In light of the Volstead Act of 1919, he made a marketing adjustment and switched to selling nonalcoholic beverages, malt and hops. Prohibition ended in 1933, and Levin went back to serving alcohol. However, later he decided to branch out and become the local beer distributor, having had a good experience representing the makers of Rheingold in the area.

Sam Levin Beer Distributor, 1961. *George Oldershaw.*

In 1943, he left his second tavern location at 92 Main Street and bought the Perry property at 87 North Bank Street. S. Levin Distributors would remain there until it was time to relocate to Crystal Avenue through redevelopment, as reported in *The Day*'s article "The Last Round" by John Foley on June 2, 1973.

Our last stop before hitting John Street is the Dudeene (named after a clay pipe from Ireland), a restaurant that during the '50s was a popular spot for league banquets, testimonial dinners, luncheons, farewell suppers and "This is your life" events with audio recordings.

On August 26, 1954, *The Day* staff celebrated their own sportswriter, Bob Nauta, with a bachelor party. He was to marry Barbara King of 15 Mather Court. Some eighty people were there to see Bob off. The parting gift was a lady's purse.

The Dudeene closed in 1960. Two years later, when it had to vacate its location on Main Street due to redevelopment, the BPOE Victory Lodge #1096 would move in before having to move again in '65 due to redevelopment. The Elks found a more permanent home at 76 Green Street, today empty.

We are now looking at the western side of the North Bank Street/ John Street intersection in 1961. On the southwestern corner stood three houses, a boardinghouse and a pre-1955 Sears Roebuck. The cleared land now serves as customer parking for the Savings Bank of New London.

The imposing structure with the mansard roof opposite is 73 John Street and 110–14–16 North Bank Street. The corner store is 110. The words on the plate-glass window say "Bernard Cohen, Delicatessen and Groceries," with all but the first three letters missing from the owner's name. (By the way, the neighboring house to the left with the full porch is 77 John Street.) Cohen ran the grocery with his wife, Rebecca. While the corner location was good for visibility, cars—or their drivers—sometimes proved an issue.

On November 26, 1954, *The Day* reported a car backing up on John Street and moving the storefront six inches farther in. On March 5, 1957, a driver maneuvering in the bank parking lot stepped on the gas instead of the brake. His right foot froze in place, shooting the car like a missile over the chain-link fence, clipping the corner grocery entrance and sailing across North Bank, barely missing a fire hydrant. Seated just inside the door with no more protection than a lawn chair, Mrs. Cohen suffered an attack on the nerves and was taken by ambulance to the hospital. She recovered and started sitting elsewhere.

Top: Dudeene Restaurant, 1961. *NLL.*

Bottom: Cohen Delicatessen, 1961. *NLL.*

Later that year, Mr. Cohen moved his grocery business to 193 Green Street, where a customer bit Mrs. Cohen's hand over an unpaid-for can of hash. The storefront at 110 North Bank remained vacant until redevelopment.

We are now at the northeast corner with John Street in early 1965. The New London News Company at 47 John Street is down at the right with the plate-glass windows. The corner building has a storefront at 109 and apartment above at 111. Note the garage in the rear that's part of the three-story brick addition, the crowning brick design. Cellar doors for easy delivery are on the left. A metal sign advertises Spur cola on the brick foundation. Canada Dry released Spur cola around 1938 and sold it in glass bottles. In 1959, the company decided to drop the cola that put "zip in every step."

109 North Bank at John Street, 1964. *CONL.*

A sign hangs in the right front window: "For Sale. Store Fixtures and Household Furniture."

For many years, Peter Mroz, the owner, lived with his family upstairs while running the grocery store down below. Peter had a brother, Frank, who kept a lobster boat on Winthrop Cove, thus ensuring his brother's customers a seasonal supply of lobster. In the mid-'50s, Peter Mros (the brothers Americanized "Mroz" to "Mros") made numerous attempts to rent the storefront and the five-room family apartment above. Except for the two years when Homer Davis used the storefront for his tool-sharpening and rental business, the store remained vacant. The apartment fared better, but nobody stayed more than a year. Shortly before 1960, Peter Mros passed on, and the building remained empty until demolition in 1966.

Seen here is the hydrant that almost stopped an errant driver in '57. This corner view now includes the smallish stucco storefront at 115 and the narrow entrance to a back apartment at 113 North Bank Street. Many of these smaller storefronts, like the modest apartments above, saw a frequent turnover in tenants. It was not unusual for a tenant to live on the same street or around the corner at five different addresses in as few as ten years. There were a variety of reasons—change in income, issues with a neighbor, issues with the landlord, running from the law or, worse, an abusive spouse.

Sometimes a landlord or lady could not wait for the rental market to place the right tenant at the right time on their doorstep. Such was the case in '54 with Mrs. Ksawera Mros, Peter's wife. She had accepted a deposit and first month's rent on the small storefront at 115 North Bank Street from a group of "gypsies" who arrived in town aboard a well-traveled Cadillac bearing New York plates. Upon setting up "shop," they placed a yard sale display of common dishes, glasses and an alarm clock minus its hands in the front window. There was the implied message that the matron of the group read palms and could foretell the future through animated gesturing. When building inspector Burton T. Gates questioned the ladies as to the lack of a certificate of occupancy for residential use in a commercial space, the women smiled politely, continued cooking with garlic and onions on the floor of the shop and asked in Spanish if the inspector had ever been to Brooklyn, as reported in *The Day* on July 13, 1954.

115, 111 and 109 North Bank. *CONL.*

One day, Gates found himself stopped in traffic on Main Street. He looked at the car in front of him: a pink Cadillac with New York plates. When traffic started to move again, he glanced at the car behind him: a canary-yellow Cadillac with New York plates. As if seeing for the first time, the inspector started noticing groups of the ladies in front of groceries and laundromats, their colorful dresses, costume jewelry and jet-black hair holding an odd attraction. On a whim that evening, he called his brother-in-law, a police desk sergeant in Williamsburg, Brooklyn.

"Gypsies? Whadda you mean, gypsies? We got bigga fish to fry down here, Burty. Just take the train down from that grease trap ya work in and I'll show ya."

Burty declined the offer and went back to his recliner and *Day* paper. Maybe the women were here as part of some kind of resettlement program for after the war?

Another group of similar global wanderers had started occupying the storefront of landlady Annie Lubow at 292 Main Street. Odd; the men always seemed to be out. A different group of ladies offered the inspector hot tea and smiles, but no answers.

A month passed. And just like that, the ladies were gone. All of them. Burty could refocus on building code violations. He looked up and down John Street. Only one Caddy did he see, and it had Connecticut plates.

If you look to the right below John Street, you can see that the Elks Club is already boarded up and awaiting demolition. The custom-made saw profile sign hanging over the shop entrance advertises another saw-sharpening business, this one run by Fred Spencer, a longtime resident of lower North Bank Street who, I'm guessing, knew Mr. Davis and quite possibly bought him out when Davis left his trade in '58. It was common for people to change their trade (groceries) for a more lucrative one (liquor) and to spend the first year or two of business living in back of or above the shop. As the availability of shops grew, these entrepreneurs packed up and moved elsewhere, even just down or across the street for a larger space or cheaper rent. Spencer lived in back of his shop. If you look closely into the shop window, you'll see a coping saw animal cartoon figure with teacup hooks, on which hangs a potholder. And not much else given the lateness of the hour.

We are now visiting 125 North Bank Street, the Gardiner-Packwood House. Thanks to Margaret W. Stacy of Waterford, *Day* staff writer, we have a good record of six historic homes facing redevelopment by way of an article she wrote that appeared in the January 28, 1965 edition of the paper around the time this photo was taken.

In 1735, Captain Jonathan Gardiner (of Gardiner's Island) had this house built on the right-hand side of Bradley Street just up from John Street. He married two years later and, due perhaps to debt, set sail for Antigua and fortune on the *Rainbow*.

The captain never came back. There was talk of a bad storm but no evidence that the *Rainbow* had met its fate therein. Captain Gardiner's newly married wife, Molly Adams, never saw her husband again and joined the other unfortunate wives and mothers on New London's "Widow's Row." Proceeds from the sale of the house in 1774 to Captain William Packwood went to Captain Gardiner's creditors.

Captain Packwood was a privateer—that is, he united with other captains in harassing the British fleet. For this purpose, he commanded the *Betsy*, a brig out of New London. On one run back to New London, the British caught up with *Betsy* and burned the ship down to its waterline. Captain Packwood and his crew escaped.

As General Arnold led his British troops forward on their three-pronged attack on New London in 1781, Captain Packwood and his men helped keep the British fleet busy while fighting nearby from the brigandine *Mary Ann*.

125 North Bank, 1964. *CONL.*

The old address for the Gardiner-Packwood House was 39 Bradley Street. After the house numbering changed around 1901, the house had three numbers: 121 for the Biliewicz-Lawski saloon, 125 for the house and 127 for a meat market. In 1913, Stephen Lawski had the brick front added and had his family helping at the bar and in the back. One of his sons, Joe, a noted athlete, remained in the house until his death in '64, whereupon his brother Walter moved in, being the last of the family to live in the house until redevelopment knocked it down in '66.

Across the street was the home of the Tamano family at 130 North Bank, a two-and-a-half-story frame house with a bricked first floor and a long vacant storefront. Val Tamano, who has worked with numerous superintendents in the New London public schools, remembers growing up on the second floor with her mom, dad and four sisters. Joe Tamano, Val's father, and I had something in common: we both drove a Blue Cab (checker) for Charlie Curtin, and we both drove "21," the number 021 on the license plate.

Val remembers, "There was a sand pile and a pull-up bar in a small lot behind the savings bank. Manny, Gladys, Anthony, some other kids and me would play Tarzan and Jane. Sometimes we would have roof races and run atop the buildings on our side of the street. At night my father would play music on the Victrola, and we would dance, dance and dance. For television we would watch the people go back and forth between Skrigan's and Peggy's Restaurant, like the Russians visiting the Poles and the Poles visiting the Russians. On Halloween we would get all costumed up and parade in the bars....People would throw money in our bags along with the candy."

When Val got a bit older, her first job was bagging bagels at Hochman Bros. Bakery at 147. Minimum wage for Connecticut in 1962 was one dollar.

Are you thirsty yet? Want to sit down and look back out on the street?

If the Dutch Tavern on Green Street had a brother, then Skrigan's at 138 North Bank Street would be that brother. There is a plaque affixed on the left side of the upper Atlantic Street entrance to the parking garage that covers most of the neighborhood like a mausoleum. Coast Guard regulars sponsored the plaque.

In the 1910s, this was Joseph Olbry's Saloon, at a time when saloons were small, numerous and generally carried the name of the owner with pride.

On Saturday, October 6, 1945, *The Day* reported on an evening of near riots at Marie's on Bank Street and Skrigan's on North Bank Street. Streams of submarine and Coast Guard sailors were back from our victory against the Japanese and, egged on by alcohol and tight quarters, looking for a fight. Today we might call this ugly mood post-traumatic stress.

Skrigan's Restaurant, 1961. *George Oldershaw.*

To my way of thinking, I don't understand how you can take a young, strong, impressionable man; separate him from loved ones, often for many months; train him to kill without a second thought for many months; and then dump him back in the United States, still far from home, and expect a full, healthy adjustment. We saw this in Korea; we saw a self-medicated response to this trauma beginning in Vietnam. Much of our social fabric was stretched to the breaking point. And here, on Bank and North Bank Streets, that fabric broke. It is a credit to the Navy Shore Patrol, the New London Police Department and the grace of God that nobody died or was seriously injured.

For the most part, however, Skrigan's was a place to relax with the homey presence of Sam Skrigan and his wife, Olga. The restaurant saw Polish bridal showers, wedding anniversaries and bachelor parties. There were isolated fights, the last one being a knife fight involving submarine sailors during the summer of '66. The incident cost Mr. Skrigan a knife cut on the face. There were no serious injuries but a workout for the two responding officers.

> *Lost and Found—brown and white puppy—lost. If found, reward. Call Samuel Skrigan, 138 North Bank St. Tel. 7041.*
>
> —The Day, *November 23, 1942*

By the late summer of 1967, Hochman's Bakery had come down and Skrigan's was left standing alone. Sam Skrigan approached redevelopment about acquiring land for a new restaurant, but nothing came of it. No demolished restaurants, to my knowledge, were rebuilt on redevelopment-cleared land. Sometime in the fall of '67, Skrigan's joined one of the nearly seven hundred home and business structures to go into a landfill, according to *The Day* of March 2, 1967.

As we cross Douglass Street and go into the next block, I want to mention one of the side effects that plagued residents and business owners who were among the first to leave the Main Street area: the stripping of buildings, both occupied and not, of their copper, brass, lighting fixtures and so on. Case in point: a woman living alone who had not yet found another place to live woke one morning to find no heat or running water in her apartment at 169 North Bank Street. Under the cover of darkness, scrappers had come and removed the basement piping. This happened in what was perhaps the largest tenement or apartment house in the city, the Soltz Block.

Each of the five sections—161, 163, 169, 171, 177—had a front and back entry with one apartment per floor. Originally the Bishop Bros. block, this wooden structure was clapboard with a slate roof and was home to fifteen families plus another family in the basement. At times, over one hundred people lived there, mostly Polish and Jewish people.

Joseph Soltz and his brother Max Soltz bought this property shortly before 1900. Both were in the kosher and non-kosher meat market business on John Street, as well as owning a saloon and meeting hall at 135 Bradley. Their nephews Lester, Alvin, Seymour and Jacob would continue the family meat trade decades later. Joseph was more of the front man in dealing with tenants, customers and rowdies. The sudden head movement of a steer cost him his sight in one eye, but you were never sure which one.

One day, the painters had just finished putting a much-needed coat of paint on the clapboards when a tenant on the third floor took the easier way and pushed a mattress out the window. Upon impact with the sidewalk, the mattress opened up, and the wind carried the feathers everywhere, covering the front of the building. It took a search party to find the tenant, reported *The Day* on April 16, 1908.

This property has an interesting past. It was originally part of a land grant bestowed on Captain John Gallup Jr. for services rendered in the colonists' fight against the Indians (later, he would die in the Great Swamp Fight

Soltz block, North Bank at Douglass. *NLPL.*

against the Narragansett tribes). In 1654, the captain sold this eight-acre plot to Peter Bradley, who built a stately home for his bride, Elizabeth (Brewster), on the Soltz block site. The property was bound by Main Street to the west, Federal Street to the north, harbor wetlands to the east and State Street to the south. A narrow lane was cleared from Main Street to the house, and this later became Douglass Street.

Peter Bradley was a mariner and loved to sail Long Island Sound. In June 1662, he set sail and never returned. Later that month, the sloop and Peter's clothing washed up in Flushing, Queens, near LaGuardia Airport.

Elizabeth thus became the first in a long line of widows on what was to become Bradley Street. However, she was not alone. A married man, Christopher Christophers, himself a landowner by upper Federal Street, had fathered two of the three Bradley children, In 1673, Elizabeth was brought before a judge, who fined her five pounds for having children out of wedlock. In addition, Elizabeth had to wear a sign stating what she had done. Three years later, the wife of Christopher Christophers died, freeing him to marry Elizabeth.

The eldest child, Peter Jr., had his father's love for the sea. And as was the case with his father, the sea took Peter Jr. away in 1697.

Peter Jr. had a son who sold the family home to Daniel Tuthill in 1730. A land surveyor, Tuthill laid out the streets and building lots. Later that year, he sold the lot with the Bradley House to John Shackmaple and Madam Sarah Shackmaple. A surveyor as well, Mr. Shackmaple was also the collector of customs for New London, a post that had brought him from England.

R.B. Wall wrote in *The Day* on November 7, 1922, that the Shackmaple family had a slave who had grown up in the household and later gained her freedom. Her name was June, and after the family line had died out, as an elderly woman, she insisted on staying in the house despite its neglected state. It was her home and she the last resident. A team of workmen pulled down the Bradley house around 1825, soon after June's death.

At what point the "highway" became Bradley Street is hard to say. In colonial records, it was referred to as the "Long highway" and then later "Second Street" due to its course paralleling Main Street and its being considered a thoroughfare as well, Carol W. Kimball reported in *The Day* on October 1, 1987.

Incidentally, the vacant lot filled with cars across the street was part of the Goddard estate and never built on. The Goddard House itself stood on the northeast corner of Douglass and Main Streets. Like many of its brethren in this area, the house had fallen into a slow decline before a wrecking crane brought it down, reported Wall in *The Day* on June 13, 1924.

Our last view of North Bank Street focuses on the west side of the street. Partially in shadow is the empty boarded-up duplex, 192–94, belonging to Julius Lovitch, who ran and lived in this rooming house with his family. During the early to mid-'50s, as reported in *The Day* on December 8, 1954, seven tenants, all on separate occasions, suffered death by asphyxiation. All were single, older men and heavy drinkers. The deaths occurred during cold months with windows tightly closed and flame space heaters left on the maximum setting. After the first two deaths, the city council considered passing an ordinance requiring an independent means of maintaining air circulation in rooming houses. Upon learning that such a measure would close up to two hundred rooms and create a shortage of single-room occupancies (SROs), the council backed off. Redevelopment would soon take care of the SROs.

Lovitch had holes put in the walls, but the boarders would stuff them with paper. In '58, Lovitch died from falling down the stairs. Up until that point, he was still renting rooms. He was ninety-one.

The red brick store bump-out at 202 North Bank was home to John's Tavern, run by Russian-born John Macule, who lived in the back.

The Minevich family lived above. Seventeen-year-old John Minevich and his classmate Michael Malinsky of 110 Potter Street made the newspaper

Upper North Bank above Douglass, 1961. *George Oldershaw.*

Sailboat *Sunray*. *From* The Day.

when Barnard L. Colby, the future *Day* publisher and grammarian, wrote a story about their almost completed sailboat and plans for racing the sixteen-foot snipe class boat. The materials cost John under fifty dollars, and with Michael's woodworking skills from Chapman Tech, it took a little over a month to build the hull behind Michael's house on Potter Street. They planned to name the boat *Sunray*.

John graduated from Bulkeley in '39, a skilled diver and lifeguard at Ocean Beach. He served in the army air corps during World War II and would later become Mr. Minevich, a widely respected and loved assistant principal at Eastern Point School in Groton, as recounted by John Foley in *The Day* on December 11, 1988.

Chapter 4

POTTER STREET

We are staying with traffic heading south from John Street to State. At the corner is 110 Potter Street, where Michael Malinsky lived while building the *Sunray* in the backyard. His mother, Annie Malinsky, kept a clean house and had relatives living nearby. One such relative, William Woroby, forgot where he was and tracked mud into the Malinsky house. Mrs. Malinsky chased the man from her house and threw a bucket of water at him. The man complained to the police, and the mother appeared before the court on a breach of peace charge. Judge Louis C. Wool fined Mrs. Malinsky ten dollars and nolled her charge against Woroby, reported *The Day* on November 1, 1954.

Left: 110 Potter Street, 1961. *George Oldershaw.*

For decades, the Soltz brothers—Jacob, Alvin, Lester and Seymour—owned and operated two meat markets, a kosher market on John Street and a nearby non-kosher market down at the corner with Potter Street, 110. Alvin ran the non-kosher market. In a discussion with a reporter about moving both markets due to redevelopment, he mentioned having work

Top: Railway Express Agency, John Street at Potter, 1961. *George Oldershaw.*

Middle: 89 Potter Street. *CONL.*

Bottom: Boss Cracker Factory (*rear*), Potter Street, 1961. *George Oldershaw.*

done years earlier at the Potter Street location. Under the building, workers had discovered hard packed white beach sand filled with fossils. In colonial times, Water Street was initially called Beach Street.

Across the street is the Railway Express Agency (REA), today's United Parcel Service or UPS. Note the cobblestones wearing through the thinning asphalt. REA had moved to a warehouse in Waterford by the mid-'60s.

Staying on the east side of Potter Street heading south is this frame apartment house at 89. The three-story brick structure next door looks like a factory but is the local maintenance facility for the New Haven Railroad. Both the railroad and city police departments used a pistol range inside the building during the '50s. Into the Penn Central era, New London remained a hub with passenger and freight traffic connections to Boston, New York, Worcester and Montreal.

As we continue walking south, we can now see the Boss Cracker Factory just past the New Haven building. At the very end, the street opens up to the back of the bus terminal. In its last decades, sailors connecting with the sub base and State Pier used this space as a parking garage. They would often come back after being away for weeks or months to find molasses had pooled on their shiny new cars.

Sam Levin started selling Rheingold on Main Street in 1912 starting with a hand truck and a will to succeed. This is the back of the W.R. Perry icehouse on North Bank Street. In the early '40s, Levin left the tavern and became a distributor.

Sam Levin Beer Distributor (*rear*), Potter Street, 1964. *CONL.*

Above: Beginning of Potter Street, 42–44 Potter in center, 1961. *George Oldershaw.*

Left: New York Harbor. *Courtesy Hudson River Maritime Museum.*

Now we are back on Atlantic Street having made the loop. Looking back up Potter Street, the Neptune Building is on our immediate left, the bus terminal our immediate right. There are holes in the streetscape where houses once were. Parking businesses like Al Baldelli's "$.50 all day parking" have sprouted.

Only one house remains near this end of Potter Street, 42–44, standing alone on the left side of the street. It belongs to Captain Michael Stokes, and he lives there with his daughter Margaret and a tenant above. Like many former neighbors, Captain Stokes was born and raised on the water—Logy Bay, Newfoundland, to be precise—and worked thirty-nine years with the marine salvage firm of Merritt, Chapman and Scott. He retired as the skipper of a lighter.

A word about the tenant who had been with the Stokes family for the past twelve years. Alice Larkin, originally of Dublin, came to the United States at sixteen on her own. Arriving in New London, she started working as a housekeeper at the Crocker House before going on to restaurant work in several places downtown. At sixty-two, Larkin was still working and living alone on the second floor.

A few days after Christmas in '58, the daughter of Captain Stokes went upstairs and discovered Larkin lying on the kitchen floor, her clothes burned off, her body covered with first-, second- and third-degree burns. A fire had burned the linoleum floor around her body. Two portable kerosene heaters stood nearby, unlit. There was no call for help, no smoke. The family dog on the first floor sensed nothing.

The job of figuring out what happened to Alice Larkin went to New London Police Detective Sergeant Dennis Murphy. His investigation of the case led him to discover that Larkin suffered from fainting spells, so he surmised that her housecoat caught on fire as she fell in a faint while refilling the heaters with kerosene. Larkin died from her wounds while unconscious, and the coroner later ruled the death accidental. In her apartment, Detective Sergeant Murphy found $339.12 of her savings.

Chapter 5

JOHN STREET

Lost and Found—Large sum of money—lost between Bulkeley School and John St. Phone 1539.
—The Day, *December 23, 1943*

John Street, if we go by the building numbers, begins at the New Haven Railroad tracks. So do Douglass and Hallam Streets. This view is toward Union Station with the large gas tank on the left and Electric Boat farther in the background across the Thames River in Groton. With good eyes, you can see the crossing tower that protected the meeting point of John and Water Streets with the railroad. A timber bridge over lower Winthrop Cove provided a connection with the Central Vermont Railway, making this an often busy location.

In the 1910s and '20s, some local residents participated in a practice we'll call "coal harvesting." Central heating was still in the future, and landlords rented "cold-water flats" where the renter was responsible for the heat and hot water. People used wood as a cheaper fuel for stoves and ovens that served the dual purpose of heating and cooking. On very cold nights, families slept not in their unheated bedrooms but in the kitchen. This was common for most, especially the new arrivals coming into New London with modest means.

Coal burns slower than wood and provides more heat, which was reason enough for steam engines to evolve from wood to coal-burning methods to heat the water into steam that pushed the pistons that moved the wheels or

Connecticut Gas Tank, New Haven Railroad tracks above Union Station, 1961. *George Oldershaw.*

drivers. Power plants, institutions, factories and large businesses used coal that arrived by rail from the mines of Pennsylvania. With the tracks of the New Haven connecting with eastern Pennsylvania, it was common to see hopper after hopper of coal in the freight consists. With traffic levels much higher than today, the New Haven had traffic jams similar to the ones we experience on I-95 and the Merritt Parkway. Very often, these train jams happened at junction points like New London, and it wasn't long before adults started boarding these hopper cars under the cover of darkness and pitching off chunks of high-grade coal the size of a softball. Children would walk the tracks and harvest the coal tossed off.

Unless there was a railroad official or policeman in the area, workers generally turned a blind eye to this practice. After November 22, 1922, that grew harder.

At the behest of the New Haven Railroad, Judge Victor Prince held a public hearing at juvenile court and had summoned to appear twenty-two boys and eight girls, charged with stealing coal tossed from halted freight trains during the early morning hours. Over fifty other children came to eavesdrop, standing in the stairwell and hallway. The judge let it be known that he would start holding parents responsible for the actions of their children when it came to trespassing and theft. He also expressed both the railroad's and the court's concern for the safety of the children. Recently, farther up in East New London, the sport of "boxcar surfing" had become popular, whereby boys and girls climbed atop moving boxcars and, with the to-and-fro rocking of empty cars, "surfed" to the sway, sudden braking and acceleration of the train. Judge Prince reminded the thirty boys and girls gathered that more than one or two unfortunate "surfers" had lost a limb.

The practice of harvesting and surfing diminished with the promised fines and support from the schools and youth clubs, reported *The Day* of November 22, 1922.

Swift Premium Meats had a small plant at 23 John Street. A railroad track served the plant, bringing in pigs by stock car and prepared meats by reefer. Vinnie Scarano remembers his father bringing deer in from hunting trips to be butchered. He also remembers workers at the plant killing the pigs with mallets as they made their way in off the loading ramp. *The Day* reported on March 28, 1957, that the work ran behind schedule and a refrigerator car waited overnight. The next morning, you guessed it—packinghouse workers found the metal seal broken, the door open and sixty-five pounds of veal sidetracked.

We are standing at Potter with the Railway Express Agency at our back. The Soltz non-kosher corner meat market is on the left. Farther up the

Swift Premium Meats, 1961. *George Oldershaw.*

View up John Street from Potter, 1961. *George Oldershaw.*

sidewalk is a sign for the Dudeene Restaurant. On the right is New London News with the plate-glass storefront run by Mr. Glassenberg. The Mros grocery with the back garage is next. The corner of Mr. Cohen's Delicatessen is visible, but Mrs. Cohen is not.

And on Main Street, we can see the back section of Beit Bros. Market and part of Sam Levin's tavern at 92 Main Street. Against blue sky, we can see the post office and the stately spire of the Second Congregational Church. In 2025, only the post office remains.

Here is New London's answer to Mystic Seaport. In this respectable lineup, we have three examples of whaling-era architecture and a turquoise and chrome rocket ship, most likely the ride of Lester Soltz, busy chatting up the customers inside. Val Tamano remembers, in the back where the prep work was done, skating on sawdust thrown down on the smooth concrete floor to absorb the blood, water and other remnants of a butcher's trade.

Going through an appeals process that eventually leads to better compensation from redevelopment, Alvin Soltz and his brothers patiently wait. They are holdouts like the Skrigans in a bleak landscape. The stores are now empty, the rocket ship is gone and the snowplow has come by for the last time.

Soltz Kosher Meat Market, 1961. *George Oldershaw.*

Three Soltz brothers holdouts, 1965. *George Oldershaw.*

On a different cold and snowy day (February 19, 1900, as reported in *The Day*), another Polish family is moving in, this time into 54 John Street, above the kosher meat market. This is Joe Soltz's house, and he is renting it. To keep warm, the family lights the oil heater. They are unfamiliar with the workings of this contraption; something goes wrong, and the heater unexpectedly flames up, igniting some bedclothes. Panic ensues. An onlooking neighbor grasps the situation and takes charge. He throws the heater and burning clothes out into the street while children shriek with terror and delight. They clap. The adults clap too. The crowd grows, surrounding and welcoming the newcomers. To the amusement of all, some of the men and women start rubbing snow on themselves. There is talk of tea.

Chapter 6

DOUGLASS STREET

We are again trackside by the bottom of Douglass Street. Aunt Bessie (Wunch), on the first floor of 177 North Bank, the Soltz block, is having a wash day, but something, according to Val Tamano, is missing—her bloomers! Aunt Bessie was a rather large gal with an equally large heart, and it was common practice for the passing New Haven road crews to look for her bloomers blowing in the breeze. Think of Baby Huey.

In the afternoon shadow of its large neighbor stands the duplex at 25. The M. Freeman kosher meat market is across the street, and the large three-story brick building at the southeast corner of North Bank and Douglass is another Soltz real estate holding, the former tavern and meeting hall.

It's 1965, and the lights are still on at Myer Freeman's kosher meat market at 24 Douglass Street. Started in 1891 by Samuel Freeman on Bradley Street, the business grew especially during the meat rationing period of World War II, when hospitals, the military and defense-related industries got first priority. Shipments of steers came in by rail as the New Haven tracks (left out of the picture) ran by the courtyard. Chickens came from local farms.

After the war, Samuel Freeman retired, and Myer Freeman took over while sons Julius and George stayed on. They worked with nephew Robert into the mid-'60s, when, unable to find another location for the slaughterhouse and storefront, they decided to close for good, according to Bob Strecker in *The Day* on January 14, 1966.

Above: 25 Douglass Street, 1961. *George Oldershaw.*

Left: Freeman Kosher Meat Market, 1964. *CONL.*

Above: Freeman Kosher Meat Market (*rear*), 1964. *CONL.*

Left: Julius, Robert and George Freeman, 1966. *From* The Day.

Not pictured is Leonard Otis, a cattle buyer and butcher who worked at 24 Douglass Street until his retirement in 1959. People may remember Otis for his team of load-pulling (eight to nine tons) oxen at state fairs. He worked with brothers Julius and George for over forty years.

So, why the name Douglass Street? Jonathan Douglass owned property on which he'd built a house on the corner of Bradley and what would later be Douglass Street. In 1734, when Jonathan died from smallpox, his brother Caleb bought the house from his widow. It is interesting to note that Frances Manwaring Caulkins in her *History of New London* cites a William Douglass as the town's packer of meats further back in 1665, a duty that included the branding and recording of all horses.

Chapter 7

MAIN STREET

The "Buttonwood Tree" stood at the northeast corner of Main (now Eugene O'Neill Drive) and State Streets. Regarded as the Charter Oak of New London, this sycamore had been standing for over one hundred years and served as a notice board for the three thousand residents who called the town home. In his photo collection on Pinterest, Fuji Fulgueras refers to the tree as the Twitter of colonial New London. Caulkins recounts in *History of New London* that when it became sick and lifeless, as shown here in front of John Strickland's provisions store, the aldermen ordered the sycamore taken down and given as fuel to the almshouse on Hill Street.

A BIG MOUTH

While we're on this corner, here's another curiosity that bears mentioning. During the '20s, '30s and '40s, a signal booth staffed by a police officer stood in the middle of the intersection. That officer handled both pedestrian and vehicular traffic. In late September 1942, a submarine base sailor became verbally abusive with the officer after being directed twice to step back onto the curb while the light was red. Brought to police court, the acting judge fined the sailor five dollars, noting that the words "Pedestrians cross only on WALK" were emblazoned on both sides of the booth. Public works employees removed the signal booth on August 14, 1952.

Left: The Buttonwood Tree, Strickland's Provisions, circa 1850. *NLPL*.

Opposite, top: Ned Gorra at the family produce store, 1968. *From* The Day.

Opposite, bottom: Lower Main Street, west side, 1961. *George Oldershaw*.

Lower Main Street had lots of shops, restaurants and offices right up until redevelopment in the late '60s. Some relocated, like Solomon's Stationery and Kaplan's Travel, but most just disappeared. Some store owners, like the Gorra family of 92 Union Street, had trouble understanding the community benefit of having their business and home taken, regardless of the payment awards. Deeb and Elizabeth Gorra, of Lebanon, had run Gorra's Fruit Market at 20 Main Street since 1921 and had passed the business along to Ned Gorra, one of four children. As the houses disappeared under redevelopment, so did the walk-in traffic. As a final phase of redevelopment in 1969, their small business was demolished to become parking for a law office and their home on Union Street for hotel parking.

My parents had their first dinner date at the Red Rose Restaurant at 14, next to Gorra's. That was in the late '40s. James Wong, a native of Canton, China, ran the restaurant during that time as well as Wong's on Truman Street, where we celebrated my ninth birthday. Wong sold the Red Rose in '56 to Arthur and Wing, who decided to close the place five months after voters approved the referendum on redevelopment in '62. The Chopsticks Restaurant opened in its place. People missed the familiar Red Rose neon sign.

California's
Finest

RESTAURANT

Left: Singer Sewing Machine, Kenney Stationers, east side, lower Main, 1964. *CONL*.

Right: Salvation Army, adjacent The Day building, 1964. *CONL*.

Singer first located on North Bank Street before moving to 19 Main Street. William Diamond was the manager and Evelyn Strekzyk the sewing instructor. Pre-redevelopment, New London offered opportunities for seamstresses and tailors in small manufactures (82 Union Street), dress shops, cleaners, laundries and at home. The Edwin Keeney Co. at 15 offered competition to Solomon's across the street, and Shu-Fix at 11 was next to Paris Cleaners.

The Salvation Army spent many decades in the handsome brick building at 43 Main Street next to The Day building. A press operations expansion at the newspaper filled the real estate void left by the demolition of the Salvation Army, Bishop Studio (35), Novitch Bros. (33), Caruso Music and Evelyn's School of Dance (29) and Turner's Flower Shop (27).

Back to the future: 2024. We are standing on the southeast corner of today's Atlantic Street, a service road for the parking garage, the bank and The Day newspaper offices and operations plant. Looking north, a two-story office addition to the bank is behind us. The Mariner Square office building is in front of us. To our left along the western side of Eugene O'Neill Drive are a series of smaller bunker-like office buildings punctuated by parking lots.

Oh, did you know that downtown had a Sears and Roebuck? Right on the corner where we are standing. In the mid-'50s, the store vacated 81 Main Street in favor of the New London Shopping Center on what would become the South Frontage Road for I-95.

Keep your eyes to the north. At one time, during the lengthy demolition phase of redevelopment, you could see clear through to Hodges Square. Let that sink in for a moment. Everything we are about to see, with the exception of Our Lady of Perpetual Help Polish Catholic Church and its rectory at the other end, will disappear.

Paul and Mary Araman lived at 97 North Bank Street by the Dudeene Restaurant. For a time, they ran Paul's Restaurant at 159 Main Street next to Maynard's Grocery. A year before the referendum, they moved their business to a larger location across from where we're standing, now the corner of John Street, at 91 Main. Like many other business owners, they kept theirs open for as long as possible until 1965, as reported in *The Day* on November 20, 1965, when redevelopment acquired the property and started charging Paul rent. Negotiations failed to find a "next move," and the Aramans ultimately lost their home and their business. New London lost as well.

Kitty's Korner at 93 is having a closing sale.

The Besenbach family lived above at 95 and rented out furnished rooms, a common practice in the redevelopment area, as it provided a cheaper alternative to staying at a hotel.

For years, Mrs. Consuelo Cornish ran Consuelo's Beauty Salon at 97. Sometime after the referendum on redevelopment sailed through, the shop became Al's Beauty Salon and in July 1964 took on two new hair stylists, Miss Susan and Miss Antoinette. Many years later, this southern practice of respectfully addressing people as "Miss" and "Mister" hit me when I moved onto South Taylor Street in Philadelphia. The children that howled in the street until ten o'clock at night called me "Mister Bill." They liked camping out on my stoop. I didn't care. My elderly neighbor did and sprinkled Ajax on her steps. She was Miss Gwen.

The three-story Rudd block follows. Barney Kosakow, an auctioneer, operated the Bargain Outlet store at 105. During the Second World War, Donald Ables operated a shooting gallery (.22-caliber) in the storefront at 109 Main Street. Up until the '38 hurricane, he'd also operated one at Ocean Beach. Eight apartments occupied the second and third floors. The Maynard family who ran Maynard's Grocery down the street lived in one of them.

Top: Paul's Restaurant, Main at John, 1964. *CONL*.

Bottom: Bargain Outlet, 1961. *NLL*.

Healy's Tavern is next at 115, the one-story brick-faced structure, run by Maurice and Catherine Healy. A pool table and dogs playing cards come to mind.

Goldie's Army-Navy Store at 119 Main (with five apartments above at 121) follows. Israel Goldstein ran the business for many years and was also the proprietor of New London & Mohegan Dairies on Jefferson Avenue. Raymond Silverman took over the store upon Goldstein's death in 1950 and then later sold everything to local auctioneer and mover of bargains Barney Kosakow in '61. In the final two years before redevelopment, the store closed and the Economy Furniture Co. occupied the storefront, most likely another Barney Kosakow operation.

The last building to complete the stretch between John and Douglass Streets on the east side of Main had a commanding presence. Before coming down (pending demolition notices are on all the doors) it had the Lee Kee Laundry at 125, four apartments above at 127 and Linda Anderson's Coffee Shop (another Main Street relocation) on the corner at 129. The Haddad

Top: Main at Douglass, lower corner, 1964. *CONL.*

Bottom: The Rivera children in front of their home at 72 Douglass Street, circa 1960. *Courtesy Manny Rivera.*

and Facas families had lived above at one time, and Anthony Facas, the father, had run a grocery store at the corner location.

The two billboards are noteworthy. The United States Air Force gives us an astronaut as a vision of the future, and Pepsi calls us to "come alive!" as part of the "Pepsi generation." In faded paint to the left is an ad for "Yee's Cafe 125 Main Street." a Chinese restaurant in business from 1944 to '45.

On the Douglass Street side at 72, Iris Rivera raised her three children, Manny, Gladys and Isabel.

In August of '61, Mr. and Mrs. Tamano gave their daughter Val a bicycle for her ninth birthday. Eddy and Patty McDermott, Manny Rivera and Anthony Facas helped celebrate.

Val Tamano's birthday, August 1961. *Courtesy Val Tamano.*

Crossing over to the west side of Main Street puts us just above Beit Bros. Supermarket at 60. Nos. 92–94 was Sam Levin's Tavern before he became a beer and soda distributor. In the '60s, this was the Ebony Lounge, a place for a dine and dance with two sets nightly. It opened in '62 under the management of Seymour Manheimer, a businessman, landlord, chair of the Star Democratic Club and all-around ear-cleaning New London cowboy. One of the first banquets hosted by Manheimer, as reported in *The Day* on September 11, 1962, was for the New London softball league postseason in September. The mayor, head of the rec department, coaches, players and their parents came. A good start.

The building was brick and had two floors of apartments above. On a warm evening in June 1963, a careless smoker in the stairwell caused a fire. Four families were smoked and watered out of a home. A ladder truck and a patient fireman rescued Agnes "Sugar" Brown from a third-floor window while a crowd of bar patrons looked on, cheering her. The Ebony Lounge reopened the next day.

On a cold wintry morning in '66, police found the front doors pried open, the two cash registers emptied, the cigarette machine coin box removed, the jukebox coin box opened and twelve quarts of liquor missing. Later that day, the Ebony Lounge reopened.

And finally, in following a trend at the movies and drive-ins for showing more skin and steam, Joe Carlin, the manager, placed a want ad in *The Day* looking for go-go girls over eighteen. Later in '68, Carlin put the Ebony Lounge up for sale.

The end came in March 1969, when Carlin, with $41,600 in liabilities and $84 in assets, went into bankruptcy after having bought the Ebony Lounge from Manheimer in June of 1967. Redevelopment took control of the property later that summer.

ROLLING WITH THE PIN CRASHERS

In this segment we pick up the story of a Main Street landmark, 126 Main Street. The Scuris Alleys (duckpin) remained at 126 Main Street until January 1970, two years after the planned wrap-up of redevelopment. The story began forty-five years earlier.

You may remember the El-n-Gee Club at 86 Golden Street, or local groups like The Reducers that played there. In 1924, the building was home to the Peerless Bowling Alleys and Billiard Parlor. On August 30, this popular business changed hands, going from Martin Iverson of New York to Peter Scuris of Thames Street in Groton.

Peter and his brother John ran a confectionary (candy, sweets) store and homemade ice cream parlor near the ferry landing (at School Street) and lived above their shop (no commute!). They promoted their business and the community through periodic food sales and boxed candy prizes in cooking contests: "Try our home-made ice cream, brick or bulk. Scuris Bros."

Peter was to be the silent proprietor of Peerless while John Nelson, of 111 Ocean Avenue, remained the manager. After a week's closure, the alleys and upstairs parlor reopened with shiny new equipment and promotions on Labor Day evening. Ten alleys awaited the leagues that had been rolling there. The place was crowded and the energy, under the new lighting, electric.

> *Pin Boys—Wanted: Peerless Bowling alleys. 86 Golden St. Apply Peter Scuris, Prop.*
>
> *—classified want ad,* The Day, *September 5, 1924*

So, what is a "Pin Boy"?

According to Joel Riley, who worked decades later at the Main Street location, a pin boy worked in the pit just beyond the pins at the end of the runway. With a pull of the lever, a dowel the size of a Bic pen would pop up above the alley surface and serve as a guide for the manual replacement of pins, each with a matching centered hole to mate with the dowel. If league teams were playing, you'd need more than one pin boy.

Now… to the dog.

On October 5, 1925, Peter Scuris placed the following classified in *The Day*: "Rabbit Hound—for sale, thoroughly broken, 3 years old; owner is unable to hunt dog and wishes to dispose of same at once. Apply to Peter Scuris, Thames St., Groton."

On October 27, the dog, Jack, reappears as the subject of a newspaper article in *The Day* describing his daily antics while fare dodging on the Mohican ferry shuttling between New London and Groton. Since the posting on the fifth, Peter had succeeded in selling Jack to a neighboring Groton bootblack (shoeshiner), Nicholas Gianacoupolas, who had a small business establishment on lower Bank Street. Nicholas had neither a gun to frighten the now gun-shy dog nor any desire to hunt rabbits.

When bored of the burlap couch afforded by the bootblack, Jack would make for the ferry at the Municipal Wharf, now known as City Pier. When a train was stopped at the station, Jack would take the footbridge over and wait calmly with the other passengers at the departure gateway. On average, this happened twice daily.

Nearing the purser, or fare collector, Jack got within petting or shooing distance and then darted off into the men's cabin, where he remained until the Mohican was well underway. Regular riders came to expect him onboard.

From the '20s on, downtown offered two other public opportunities to bowl duckpin: the YMCA on Meridian and Arthur Simpson's lanes at 17 Bank. All three stayed busy with leagues and three-player teams sporting such names as the Dark Horses, the Question Marks, the Polish Falcons and the Alley Cats. Some of these players shared a common living, as did the Meter Readers, the Grocers, the Butchers and the Bankers, while others shared a common place, like the Crystal Avenue Sluggers, the Sub Station, Electric Boat Night Shift or Hammy's.

Top: The Mohican ferry, circa 1925. *Courtesy Jim Streeter.*

Bottom: Onboard the Mohican ferry, Groton Landing. *Jim Streeter.*

Hogan's Alley, captained by a Morse, often played the Gopher Feathers, skippered by a MacDonald. Many decades would pass before a similarly named pair, this time leading the Scrubbers and the Over 100 Club, would periodically crash pins at Simpson's.

Six hundred fans turn out for the grand opening of Scuris Alleys at its new location, 126 Main Street, opposite the Olympia Tavern, diagonally across from Douglass Street. It's Saturday night, August 21, 1937. A dozen new Brunswick lanes. Air conditioning. Special, bring-them-in first-week rates. Smiles, cigars and glad-handing all around.

Mayor Leo Reagan has the honor of rolling out the first ball. He removes his jacket, revealing a vest and pocket watch, revealing a growing paunch from too much "sit time" listening and reading, listening and reading. There's a nonverbal sigh in his bull-like body that no longer intimidates. He rolls up his sleeves to reveal silver cufflinks with a whaling ship. The mayor likes to sail, alone if possible, eyeing the city he loves from a comfortable distance. No questions, no fights; just seagulls looking for food.

The mayor throws, a bit awkwardly. Fast and determined, the ball slams into the gutter. The crowd roars its approval. Money changes hands. Some choice words for His Honor. The next throw clips two off the right, the third, three off the left. More money, more choice words. The mayor forces a smile and plops down.

City Manager John Sheedy strides forward, waves to no one in particular and picks up a ball. Puts it down. Pauses. Picks up another. The back of his white shirt sticks to his skin. The air conditioning can't handle the crowd, the heat. The mayor smiles to himself and looks up at a ceiling fan, the blades moving in the wrong direction. The city manager picks a third ball, holds it before him, corrects his posture and, at the end of a perfectly geometric swing, lets the ball go. Someone yells from the back, "A Joe Cranker roundhouse!" The local star pitcher with a record of thirteen strikeouts would be proud. Hands on his hips, Sheedy watches the pins explode, then nods. He has just won himself a week's salary. Flasks get passed around. The pool going around gets fatter, nears $500. It's gonna be a great night.

The seasons come and go. People win, people lose. In '61, the alleys are closed for a month due to remodeling. It's time to bring the Scuris Alleys into the '60s. The Kozy Korner league is forming again for its third season.

On July 13, 1967, news of the inevitable comes out after five long years of redevelopment. The federal government under the Department of Housing and Urban Development approves a plan to demolish twenty-five remaining businesses along the west side of Main Street and a section of State for a final thrust into the city's heart. They are:

1. The Stemma Club of New London
2. Carlson's Liquors
3. Chopsticks (Red Rose) Restaurant

4. Gorra Fruit Market
5. Kaplan's Shoe Department
6. Solomon Stationery
7. California Fruit and Produce
8. The Brainard Building
9. The Hull Building
10. Beit Bros. Supermarket
11. The Ebony Lounge
12. Hammy's Restaurant

Plus:

13. The Half Hour Laundry (interestingly, no laundromats were left for the new residents)
14. Moutran Real Estate (with no new owner-occupied housing, who will need to buy a house?)
15. John Prentis Blueprints
16. Robinson's Barbershop (men are growing their hair long anyway)
17. Golden Rod Restaurant
18. Main Street Billiards (you can drive to Crown Billiards at the shopping center near Bradlees)
19. Globe Spirit Shop (there's another one on Green Street.)
20. John's Sandwich Shop (there'll be a Subway eventually at State and Bank)

And of course:

21. P. Scuris Bowling Alleys (go to Simpson's if you need to bowl)

Lest we forget the hit that State Street was about to take:

22. The Four Winds Book Shop (go to the library)
23. Salem V. Smith's Beauty Clinic and Real Estate Office
24. M-A-C Loans
25. Big L Cosmetics

Of those businesses listed, only John Prentis (Winthrop Center by the Salvation Army), Solomon's (Bank Street), Kaplan's (State Street) and California Fruit (in the A&P) would relocate. The others were done. Welcome to the '60s.

During the final two years, Pete Scuris tried to enjoy some form of retirement while his passion and livelihood slowly ran out of steam under the dark cloud of pending demolition and a growing scarcity of neighbors. Dust and noise were everywhere. Drivers avoided the area. They went to the shopping center, the new mall on the interstate and the quieter, less in-your-face excitements of easy-to-reach Waterford.

And yet, there were some high points. As the Christmas of 1968 approached, New London Lodge of Elks sponsored 150 youngsters, ages eight to sixteen, in a duckpin tournament that brought in a lot of smiles and excitement belying the desolate, empty surroundings. In June of '69, the Bridgeview barber, Mario Strafaci, having lost his earlier location at 815 Main Street to the wrecking ball, moved in next door at 218. Later that year in September, the start of the '69–'70 bowling season, the Kooler League announced its first meet with a social hour to follow.

The season ended short. In January 1970, the city, acting on behalf of redevelopment, took title to 216 Main Street and Scuris Alleys. At about this time, Peter Scuris fell ill and was cared for by his wife, Helen.

In February, the agency wiped out $2,880 in back rent owed them by Peter, a legal arrangement that allowed the alleys to stay open just a bit longer.

In March, Pete Sepowitz, of Uncasville, beat the Scuris record of a three-string score of 472 set in 1936, with a new record of 476 set at Simpson's on lower Bank.

On September 5, the start of the '70–'71 season, *The Day* published the obituary of Peter Scuris, who passed on after a nine-month illness. In December, a photo of him and John appeared in the "Only Yesterday" posting, taken in 1918. It shows the store interior, the two young men and four employees all in white smocks, waiting as if for a summer crowd getting off the ferry eager for a fountain drink, homemade ice cream or a bag of sweets.

WHERE IS JACK?

Head back across to the east side of Main Street, still heading north toward Federal Street. Once called the Moutran House, the history of this barn-like building goes back to the mid-1700s, when the Sons of Liberty met in what was the Fox and Grapes Tavern. At 153 is the office of Moutran (George) Realty. Jack and Lila Maynard ran a grocery at 157, where their daughter Elaine remembers dozens of grinders going out for sub launching events and an all-seeing elf watching her and the store from behind a failing ceiling tile above the cash register. And there was that friendly sub officer who brought them back a lace tablecloth and napkins set after a lengthy deployment in Ireland.

Maynard Grocery, 1961. *George Oldershaw.*

John Blanos, a World War I army veteran born in Tripoli, Greece, owned and managed John's Sandwich Shop for more than twenty-five years at 165 Main across from Church Street (Governor Winthrop Boulevard). Concetta "Connie" Spinnato worked as the cook in the kitchen. Connie came to New London at age twelve from Tusa, Sicily, and would later become president of the Tusana Ladies Society, a group that often held events at the Mohican Hotel ballroom.

At times, the two dealt with difficult customers. One evening, a man came into the restaurant, sat at the counter and demanded a steak dinner. When asked if he had the money for such a meal, the man plunked down three pennies and threatened to come back with others if not served a steak. "I'm not running a charity," John replied and called the police. The next day, the man appeared in police court charged with intoxication and breach of peace before Judge Wool. The judge fined the man five dollars on the drunk charge and ten dollars on the breach of peace charge. Unable to pay either, the man went to jail. Dinner that night was not steak.

On the left, out of the picture, was 171, the former grocery of Mr. P.J. Haddad and later, in the '50s, Mr. Mounir Shakkour. Three apartments were above.

We continue walking down the east side of Main toward Federal Street. There's another barn-like structure from another century: the Red Lion Inn.

Left: John's Sandwich Shop, 1964. *CONL.*

Below: Red Lion Inn, 1964. *CONL.*

Opposite: Nahas Grocery, 1964. *CONL.*

According to Margaret Stacy, staff writer for *The Day*, Captain Nathaniel Coit was one of the original owners, having retired from trade runs to Ireland and the West Indies to settle down and run the tavern. And yes, George Washington did sleep here while in his twenties during the French and Indian War in 1756. It was also called the Belden House.

The Bonacci family owned the Red Lion. At 189, Edmondo Bonacci operated a shoe store and at 193 a clothing store. Both are empty. A brazen daylight armed robbery at the clothing store that netted $200 and later jail time for the two suspects may have been the last straw for the owners, according to *The Day* of June 8, 1965.

Before redevelopment, Solomon Nahas operated a grocery at 197. His wife, Frieda, was the manager. Upstairs at 195, you could get a furnished room from the Bonacci family with fresh coffee and a pastry waiting downstairs. But not after 1967.

We're at the last three businesses before hitting Federal Street. The Charles Lee Laundry is on the right at 199. For the last couple of years before redevelopment, this was the Christopherson Plumbing office. The Star Barber Shop at 201 belonged to George Telage, a former weaver who come to New London via Willimantic and Lebanon. His health began to fail during an appeal over the award (compensation) amount for his

Above: Jigg's Package Store, Talmadge Barber Shop, 1964. *CONL.*

Left: Crown Cleaners, 1964. *CONL.*

Opposite: View from Jigg's toward Schneider Hardware, Church Street, 1961. *George Oldershaw.*

property in the spring of '65. Telage passed that same year in September. The private viewing box over Main Street was the domain of the Blanco family at 203 Main Street. Tenants for almost a dozen years, they would be the last. Mary Joyal operated Jigg's Package Store at 207. Older readers may remember Maggie and Jiggs from the newspaper comic strip *Bringing Up Father*. Much like the Bumsteads in *Dagwood*, Jiggs and Maggie never aged and seemed to prefer living in the flapper age. Mrs. Joyal, however, faced the mid-'60s and would soon leave and relocate her business on Howard Street close to Bank.

Federal Street before redevelopment ran across Main and down to connect with North Bank. Walk across Federal to the other side. We are now in front of Crown Cleaners and the apartments at 215–17 Main Street.

Look back along the west side of Main Street toward Church Street. This is what we've missed. With good eyes, you can make out the Den Restaurant (Coca-Cola sign) run by Jack Holmes at 144 Main under the Sterling Salt roof billboard. The Globe Spirit Shop on the far corner of Church Street belonged to Seymour Manheimer. The Capital Service Station on the near corner offered gas at twenty-seven cents a gallon. George Clion operated N.Y. Shoe Repair at 188, and Dorothy Summerscale managed the Glamour Beauty Shop at 190 with the help of Helen Przelomiec. The J.J. Schneider Hardware Company has been at 198 Main Street since 1928; it would later relocate to Bank Street. And finally, the Polish American Progressive Club is on the corner of Federal at 206. Stanley Zukowski was the club's steward.

Standing on the northwest corner of Federal and Main at 230 is Sebastian Lawrence's 1850 villa, now the B.P. Learned House under the direction of John Kashanski. Let's cross the street and take a closer look at the villa.

This playground is on the site of another, very similarly designed villa that was taken down in the '50s. Under the umbrella of "Associated Charities," it was the home of the New London Day Nursery, the Visiting Nurses Association and other community groups.

Before the building came down in '67, redevelopment used the villa as a field office. The parlor had a white marble fireplace. Local watercolor artist Roger Dennis caught the last day.

As we continue our stroll along the west side of Main Street toward Hodges Square, we come across another pesky old building standing in the way of New London's march into the '60s. This one is called the Woodbridge House opposite Hallam Street. The house was built in 1769 by Nathaniel Shaw for his daughter Mary and her new husband, the Reverend Ephraim Woodbridge, who etched on a windowpane the following: "Ephraim Woodbridge. Hic Vixit. Hail happy day! The fairest sun that ever rose. 1769."

The British marched past the house in 1781 without touching it, for they were far more interested in burning the warehouses on Hallam Street, then called the Town Wharf. In 1961, the above apartments were at 262, an auto parts dealer at 264 (look closely,

Opposite, top: B.P. Learned House (former Lawrence villa), 1961. *George Oldershaw.*

Opposite, middle: Main Street side of B.P. Learned House. *George Oldershaw.*

Opposite, bottom: Learned House windows. *George Oldershaw.*

This page, left top: Learned playground on the site of the former Miner villa. *George Oldershaw.*

This page, left bottom: The Learned House's white marble fireplace. *George Oldershaw.*

This page, below: Learned House demo, 1967. *Roger Dennis Collection, Lyman Allyn Museum.*

Woodbridge House, 1961. *George Oldershaw.*

the Coleman Bros. Show was in town), State Venetian Blind at 268, more apartments at 270 and L.E. Robinson's Barbershop and Supplies at 272 and 274. Redevelopment took down the Woodbridge House in 1966.

One building remains on this block, an early frame apartment house with two storefronts. Both W.H. Baum and D.W. Small were landlords and had real estate and insurance offices here at 278 Main Street. Lucille's Rib Hut operated out of the last storefront on the block for a couple of years, and then Weezie's Restaurant or Kitchen held the corner until late '64. If you know more about Lucille or Weezie, please send me an email. Thank you.

This brings us to Shapley Street, a bit steeper than Church and Federal Streets in climbing the hill from Main to Huntington Street. The early three-story brick building was the home of Captain Stevens Rogers, a sailing master instrumental in making the 1819 Atlantic crossing a first for a steam/sail vessel. In just twenty-two days, using both steam and sail (to conserve coal), the *Savannah* sailed/steamed from Savannah, Georgia, to Liverpool, England, and later on to Stockholm, Sweden, and St. Petersburg, Russia. In the 1850s, the captain retired from the sea, lived in this brick home and worked as a customs agent collecting taxes. Captain Stevens Rogers, born in Great Neck (Waterford), passed in 1868, recounted *The Day* on April 25, 1919.

Top: Captain Stevens Rogers House, 1961. *George Oldershaw.*

Bottom: The *Savannah. Courtesy the Frank L. McGuire Maritime Library, New London Customs House.*

Abe Gordon ran this and other Yellow Front package stores in New London. He initially got his start in the grocery business on North Bank Street during the '20s and later saw more opportunities selling beverages. Next door at 292 Main is Wimpy's Shoe Shine Parlor. Judging from the altered signage and the cigarette sales stickers in the windows, this may have earlier been a grocery, though Mason's Restaurant made the paper at this location in '56 due to a teenage brawl involving a ketchup bottle, as reported in *The Day* on January 3, 1956.

In the next building at 308, Ezell "Tommy" Strong operated a barbershop. The Navy and World War II brought Strong from Texas to New London. He married Barbara from Old Mystic, and over the late '40s and early to mid-'50s they had four children. One son met with a fatal truck accident at the age of four, and another grew up to be a commercial fisherman on the West Coast. Along with Mr. and Mrs. Baum, Tommy and his wife were active members of the New London chapter of the Progressive Republican Club. Tommy also dabbled in real estate, notably with restaurants in the '40s, such as Kat's Chicken Shop on Main Street. When redevelopment came to 308, he moved his barber business to 77 Blinman Street, calling it the Columbus Barbershop. An avid reader, Tommy also enjoyed playing cards with wagers on the side.

This last building on the block could date from 1790. At 320 Main was King's Fish Market in the '30s and the Harlem Restaurant in the '40s. You went upstairs to the five apartments by the central doorway at 322. The last storefront on the block was home to the IGA City Market in the '30s and '40s. Rose and Willy Nahas operated the Main Street Market here in the early '50s before selling the business to Wilbur and Hazel Cheney. David Telage, our barber friend from 201 Main Street, bought the building in '61 and started renovations, which entailed combining the two storefronts and dressing them up with a brick veneer.

In April the following year, voters approved redevelopment, and the renovation work stopped. A faulty space heater in the Ellis family apartment above burned out the apartment shortly before Christmas, reported *The Day* on December 14, 1962. Careless cigarette smoking and faulty or improperly used space heaters had been a scourge in apartment houses for decades; however, the fire department started reporting an uptick in Main Street–area fires after April's referendum.

320 Main Street at Hill, 1961. *NLL.*

RESTLESS NIGHTS

On Saturday night, November 20, 1943, Miss Mattie Ross of 312 Main had finished dancing with James Hall, who danced next with Mrs. Rose Land. Ross and Hall left the Harlem Restaurant together. Land followed them out onto the sidewalk and, according to Miss Ross, pulled a pistol from her purse and threatened to shoot. Hall claimed to see a shiny object between the two women and stepped between them. Land turned abruptly away and marched home.

Upon a complaint from Ross, police arrested Land and charged her with carrying a concealed weapon. Her attorney, Morris Lubchansky, claimed in police court that the shiny object was nothing more than a cigarette lighter/holder that Land kept in her handbag. The judge issued a $1,000 bond to be posted and instructed the police to locate the alleged pistol within the next twenty-four hours or have the case thrown out. The police were unable to turn up any gun, and the judge threw out the case, according to *The Day* of November 22, 1943.

The Day reported on October 28, 1943, that at half past midnight, John Smith, manager of the Harlem restaurant at 320 Main Street, entered into a fight, trying to eject an intoxicated sailor from the restaurant after the sailor had started tearing latticework from the booths. The fight continued out onto the sidewalk. People gathered. The police and shore patrol arrived, arrested the sailor and started dragging him to the station. More people gathered and followed as the police and shore patrol continued their struggle with the sailor. The sailor begged the onlookers to intervene, and women in the crowd egged the men on to do something. The crowd became a mob of over one hundred people surrounding the two men, demanding they release the sailor. The policeman stayed with the sailor while the shore patrol ran to a callbox for help. Two other police officers arrived, and the crowd slowly dispersed. Judge Boyer fined the sailor five dollars for public intoxication and ten dollars for resisting arrest and sentenced him to twenty days in the Franklin Street jail, known by some as the "winter resort."

We are now crossing Hill Street on cobblestones laid down 150 years earlier from horse-drawn carts. There is a smallish single-story brick appendage on the corner, now boarded up. This tiny bump of commerce, 336 Main Street, has been a shoe repair shop (M. Chojnowaki) and a package store with more than one owner. In '38, it belonged to Stephen J. "Zeke" Czekala, who later moved his beverage business down to the corner of Richards Street at 424 Main. In the '40s, it was a short-lived men's social club that was social in that drinking and gambling are more interesting with other people.

Russell "Tip" Merrill operated this "gambling resort" at 336 just after the war in '45. A police raid netted fifteen men, several of whom were Navy and Coast Guard. The early morning raid succeeded when an electric alarm system used by a doorman to "tip off" players in the back room was left unattended. In a further adjoining room, a crowd of men and women were enjoying a cocktail party, reported *The Day* on September 8, 1945.

The large apartment house, or "big brother," had two storefronts. At 338, Jack Holmes operated a pool hall in the early '50s before acquiring the Den Restaurant at 144 by Church Street. Jamaican-born Cyril and Phyllis Hylton operated the Imperial Restaurant at 342 during the '40s and afterward started a charity that benefited the Hillside Home on Garfield Avenue, a city-run home for the destitute that served some thirty men and women. The Hyltons also became landlords in the neighborhood. Linda Anderson was the next tenant and would wind up moving her coffee shop twice due to redevelopment. *The Day* reported on May 27, 1958, about Maxine Clark celebrating her tenth birthday at a surprise party at Linda's. Twenty-four fourth graders from Jennings School helped Maxine mark the occasion.

The old Phillips House at 358–62 had a brick first floor and housed the Star Tavern in the late '30s and Alphonse Fletcher's pool hall around 1960. In the second half at 362, you'll find the IBOE (Elks) World Victory Lodge #1096. This is where the Imperial Carib Club, "Ma" Hylton's civic group,

Left: Looking up Hill Street from Main, 1964. *CONL*.

Opposite, top: Zeke's at Richards Street, 1961. *NLL*.

Opposite, bottom: The Parsonage, 1961. *NLL*.

would hold its Christmas party to benefit Hillside Home. James Taylor was steward of the Elks.

Whaling City Ford filled out the rest of the block to Richards Street. Older New Londoners may remember the Model T Ford on the roof. With redevelopment, Sigmund Strochlitz moved his business to Colman Street and expanded, consolidating his new and used car and truck offerings. The J. Spaulding plant nursery was at this location fifty to one hundred years earlier. John Spaulding was a pioneer commercial florist.

On the northwest corner of Richards and Main stands a three-story frame apartment house built into the hill. Zeke's Package Store has been here since '38 after Stephen J. Czekala moved the business from the corner of Hill and Main Streets. Previous tenants were grocery and meat markets. Joseph Hoff had such a market in the 1910s, and when he wanted to move his beverage trade from Atlantic to 424 Main Street, the two judges and others on the liquor commission panel overruled him on grounds that the immediate vicinity was purely residential. The area changed in the ensuing years, and Zeke moved in.

We are now standing before the former parsonage of the First Congregational Church at 450–52 Main Street. There was physical evidence that this large two-door house was once two separate houses, the first built in 1740 and the second in 1753. The congregation sold the parsonage, or "glebe," in 1849 and used the proceeds to buy the building lot at State and Union for what would eventually be the First Congregational Church. Tragically, a critical flaw in the building of the steeple would lead to a collapse in early 2024, making necessary a complete demolition of the church.

The parsonage had two six-room apartments on the top floor and two five-room apartments on the bottom. It passed from the estate of Charlotte C. Ross of Newark to a daughter named Ruth in the '50s and from Ross to redevelopment in '65.

A PORTAL ON MAIN STREET?

Ronald M., a crew member of the submarine *Dogfish* at the State Pier, had no explanation when police found him in a North Bank Street apartment house hallway clothed only in a flour sack and one sock. At police headquarters, he recounted that he remembered walking down Main Street and…that's it. This lack of memory cost him an eighteen-dollar fine, reported *The Day* on September 10, 1962.

We are looking back along the west side of Main Street. Where Eastern Auto Body stands at 464 Main was the site of Judge Mather's family home dating back to 1791. Like many other named, older houses, it was cut up into private rooms and turned out a very modest profit that couldn't keep up with the required maintenance of a large wooden house. In thirty years, the judge's home went from jewel to eyesore. By 1931, it was gone.

In the background is the glebe house and, farther back, the apartment house above Zeke's Package Store at the corner with Richards Street.

We are standing at the start of Crystal Avenue on the east side of Main looking north toward the bridge. Before redevelopment, Winthrop Cove was more expansive. In late '66, more than four years after the referendum approval, redevelopment was still trying to figure out if the cove was a liability or an asset. It is important to remember that the general attitude toward wetlands was different than today. Just as civic leaders saw the old buildings and the people who lived and worked in them as an impediment to progress, so did they perceive wetlands. Hence, much of the cove would be filled in and fenced off.

Farther down Main toward the bridge on the left-hand side is Stony Hill. Unlike the other side streets, Stony Hill reaches up to Huntington Street on a diagonal veering off to the south. Seafarers who made their homes on this steep and narrow lane must have enjoyed the harbor views to the southeast.

Opposite Stony Hill, Larry and Joseph "Pullie" Gomez lived with their family at 579 Main Street. They were considered "Black Portuguese," having come from the Cape Verde Islands off the west African coast. The brothers worked off and on at the State Pier. Both boxed and never shied from drama. On one occasion, Larry and Pullie took on "half the fleet" at the Den Restaurant over something that didn't make the paper (reported on October 13, 1951). They walked away. Others did not. Judge Wool fined them twenty-five dollars apiece for breach of peace and gave them six months' probation.

Top: Eastern Auto, site of the former Mather home, 1961. *George Oldershaw.*

Middle: Upper Winthrop Cove, 1961. *George Oldershaw.*

Below: Main Street at Stony Hill, 1963. *Roger Dennis Collection, Lyman Allyn Museum.*

Now it's the summer of '64. City health director Dr. Charles Dyer has condemned the apartment house at 579 as unfit for human habitation. John Miga Jr., fifty-seven, a longshoreman, and Lena Correlli, sixty, a housekeeper, were neighbors who became friends. They were sharing an apartment in the building. Following the health director's instructions, the police ordered the couple to leave.

Summer slides into fall. The police discover John and Lena still in their apartment and order them to leave a second time. When they refuse to leave, the police arrest them for failure to leave an unsanitary dwelling. Hillside Home takes the couple in, and the police drop the charges, as reported in *The Day* of November 13, 1964.

Rose Shankel ran the Home Hand Laundry from her home at 669 Main Street, where she'd been since 1900. (Note the drying sheets behind the house in the middle.) On May 13, 1962, weeks after voters approved redevelopment through a referendum, New London High School hosted a Mother's Day program in honor of Shankel. Spencer Lancaster of the board of selectmen and the Reverend A.A. Garvin, pastor of Shiloh Baptist Church, officiated. One hundred persons were in attendance to celebrate Shankel as a role model for the community and to support the church's building fund. Her son, Jimmy Shankel, a well-known boxer and trainer in the amateur realm known as Young Joe Gans, was a lightweight and then a welterweight. He sent out a challenge through *The Day* sports pages to take on Cowboy Sheehan and Bruce Sloan. Not sure of the response.

Prescott Bush, former U.S. senator from Connecticut, and his wife, Dorothy Walker Bush, were also in attendance at the event. Mrs. John Lodge, the former actress and ballet dancer, and Francesca Braggiotti, now wife of the former Connecticut governor, were there to present Shankel with a portable television set. Judge Angelo Santaniello had come, as well as Mayor Harvey Mallove. The mayor made a point of thanking church members for their help in getting redevelopment approved on R-Day through the referendum. He also noted that success in redevelopment would depend on continued active support in relocating residents and businesses out of the Winthrop Cove area.

Shankel, her house and her business would be gone in less than two years. Dorothy Walker Bush shared some parting words from the Mother's Day tea at the high school: "Connecticut has always respected the Constitution, granting equal rights to all."

Located across the street from the Shankel house is Al's Dug Out at 672, with a step-down counter service offering grilled food. Albert and Concetta

Top: Upper Main Street from the bridge, 1961. *George Oldershaw.*

Bottom, left: Mrs. William H. Baum, Mrs. Rose B. Shankel and Mrs. Edward H. Green, 1960. *From* The Day.

Bottom, right: Upper Main Street, Mill Street on left, 1961. *George Oldershaw.*

Pongetti ran this non-chain fast-food joint, a convenient favorite among nearby Winthrop School teachers and students.

That same year, the Electra Chapter of the Order of the Eastern Star celebrated Shankel with its own Mother's Day tea at the Hempstead Hall at 66 Hempstead Street.

This will be our last glimpse at Main Street circa 1961. By way of Mill Street at the lower left, we will loop around on Winthrop and, via Crystal Avenue, reconnect with Main and go up Stony Hill.

Chapter 8

WINTHROP STREET

Lost and Found—Boat—Lost, 12 ft. rowboat, red bottom, blue sides, gray inside, racks on floor. Was in Winthrop Cove. Call 3-7217
—The Day, *August 22, 1953*

Winthrop Street, as the name implies, parallels the eastern side of Winthrop Cove (both named for Connecticut's first governor, whose home stood by Winthrop School), offering property owners generous backyards down to the water. In our unobstructed view from the bridge, we can see Lewis Street directly below on the left and, farther down, Front Street, also on the left. Just beyond our view, Winthrop Street crosses Crystal Avenue. We will take a right on Crystal, rejoin Main, take a short right and head up Stony Hill.

We are standing on Lewis looking at what was, until recently, 132 Winthrop Street. A bulldozer is filling a dump truck with the smashed remains. A boy surveys the scene, watching the cleanup from behind the former front porch roof. Did he know the people who lived in this house, possibly have a classmate on the second floor, now moved away? Or is this a summer day and Dad has brought his son along to work?

Stephen Kuzia, a contractor, built this house at 118 Winthrop and a similar one at 110 Winthrop. They are cinder block houses with a stucco finish. Charles Potter Sr. had recently bought and moved into 110, opposite Front Street. The referendum passed, and the first houses to go were on Winthrop Street, with the circa 1826 two-story Misarski house at 100 first.

Top: Bridge view of upper Winthrop Street, 1961. *George Oldershaw.*

Bottom: Demo of 124 Winthrop opposite Lewis Street, late 1962. *George Oldershaw.*

118 Winthrop Street, 1961. *NLL.*

Mayor Richard Martin was there with a small crowd of onlookers as the bulldozer spent a little over fifteen minutes clearing away the home.

"I am delighted with the possibilities of new and more modern housing facilities and ideas and plans for increased employment and new industrial facilities." As reported in *The Day* of September 6, 1963, the mayor went on: "This area presently houses about 60 families. Within 18 months we hope to see public housing for 125 families."

The Misarskis, the Kuzias and the Potters didn't want to live in a "housing facility"; they wanted to live in a home. For all the owner-occupied housing bulldozed under redevelopment, not a single owner-occupied home was built. This trend would continue in other New London redevelopment efforts.

The Wilkinson Grocery at 75 stood on the northeast corner of Winthrop and Crystal, the Polish American Club across at 80. The sign in the window says, "This is our last week. Store closing November 2nd [1963] due to redevelopment." A young couple is bowling on the small billboard advertisement: "Now it's Pepsi for those who think young."

Left: Wilkinson Grocery, 1964. *CONL.*

Below: Winthrop School, 1964. *George Oldershaw.*

With the clear-cutting, it was now possible to see Winthrop School from Crystal Avenue. Note the laundry on the line to the right. The noise and the dust were further reason to leave. Few wanted to live in the last house standing.

The Winthrop Elementary School stood on Mill Street under the reverberations and pounding of trucks and cars overhead. For a time, it was unsettling to see classmates disappear, one by one. And then a second span

Winthrop School, 1961. *George Oldershaw.*

Crystal Avenue high-rises (three), 1978. *George Oldershaw.*

High-rise site, 2024. *Author.*

was built and the school disappeared. (Vinnie Scarano and Peter Detmold were students.)

We're sitting on a bench in the courtyard of a housing facility. Within weeks of opening in 1967, the elevators were broken, doors wouldn't close let alone lock and the wading pool was a catch basin for wind-blown trash. The asphalt and cinder block walls required less maintenance. It is now 1978, judging by the artistic attempt to soften the hard edges of the place. Another mayor visited the site on opening day. "This place is beautiful," he gushed.

Open skies and equally open land. Today, the site sits empty. Water still flows from the Old Town Mill to Winthrop Cove and, by extension, the Thames River. There is a wonderful opportunity here to bring people and nature back together and make this a desirable place once again to play, work and live. Any ideas?

STOP THE PRESS!

Through a chance encounter at a fiftieth high school class reunion, I ran into Miss Rayna of the Duggan-Rossi clan who lived in the '50s and early '60s on Harrison Street, which is where Winthrop Street began. At this corner was a flatiron type of triangular three-story building called Max's Tavern at 15. I think this short detour will prove interesting.

In the 1910s, this was the Dennis A. Doyle Saloon until Prohibition in 1920. Doyle continued living above on the second floor with his family and became a policeman. One afternoon, while he was walking toward downtown along the Central Vermont rail/foot bridge crossing Winthrop Cove, a dog ran up to him barking furiously. The policeman ran with the dog along the bridge, and about halfway across, the dog stopped. Doyle looked over the railing and, under a workman's plank, saw a four-year-old boy in the water beneath, his older brother and a friend gone. A red polo cap was pulled tightly over the boy's head. Climbing down, the policeman scooped up the boy by his clothing and carried him to the warmth of John Davey's blacksmith shop just past the end of the bridge. The boy recovered in the shop, and Doyle took him home. Later in life, Dennis Doyle worked on the trains of the Central Vermont and New Haven Railroads. He also served on New London's board of selectmen, an elected position.

Max's Tavern, 1961. *George Oldershaw.*

It was toward the end of Prohibition in 1931 that Max Apanaschik of Minsk opened his restaurant next to the old Doyle Saloon. The Doyle Saloon became the Sea Gull Tavern for a few years after Prohibition ended in '33. In '37, Max and his wife, Nastarie, closed the restaurant, and the International Longshoremen's Association moved in and would remain until redevelopment had the building demolished in the summer of '65. The Sea Gull closed and reopened in '38 as (Antoni) Worobey's Tavern. Max Apanaschik took over in '43 and renamed the place Max's Tavern. Like the longshoremen, he would remain in place until redevelopment. He was friends with Sam Skrigan, a fellow Russian who, if you remember, ran his own tavern on North Bank Street along with his wife, Olga. Their sons, Henry Apanaschik and Paul Skrigan, played basketball together at Bulkeley School in the late '30s. Both taverns offered changing food menus, live music and dancing. Max's offered a talent show on Sunday evenings from five to seven o'clock. And like all taverns, it served beer and wine only.

Across from Max's was a small playground for the kiddies. Miss Rayna remembers her mom taking her and her brother Michael there and how

Lower Winthrop Cove, 1961. *Right to left, foreground*: Central Vermont Railway track/ foot bridge, John Davey's blacksmith shop (above boats); *above, right to left*: Captain Stevens Rogers House (brick building), Sidney Manufacturing, Woodbridge House (Ahavath Chesed above), B.P. Learned House, Mohican Hotel, Brainard & Armstrong smokestack, Crown Cleaners, First Congregational Church. *George Oldershaw.*

they would deliberately cross Winthrop Street from Harrison on the other side opposite the tavern. Both the Duggan and the Rossi sides of the family lived around the corner and up the hill at 24 Harrison Street, a two-family, two-and-a-half-story cedar-shingled house with a front porch and side yard. Miss Rayna's mom stayed at home, and her father, Raymond, a high school dive and swim champ familiar with the Ocean Beach pool and later a Korean War army vet, worked as a third-generation locomotive engineer with the neighboring Central Vermont Railway. Many in the neighborhood either worked for the CV or had jobs at the State Pier, a five-minute walk. Looking south from their street gave you an interesting view of lower Winthrop Cove and Main Street beyond.

Chapter 9

STONY HILL

We are once again on Main Street after having circled back along Crystal Avenue. On the west side of the street, a lane ascends the hill leading up to Huntington Street. This narrow thoroughfare is called Stony Hill.

Here we see a Christmas card view as we start our march up Stony Hill, once called "Codner's Highway" (Edward Codner was a mariner who first showed up in 1651) and "Featherbed Lane" (sarcasm).

The snow has now melted away, and it's spring (or early summer) on a Sunday morning in 1961. Looking up along the north side of the narrow street are 9, 13, 17 and 19 Stony Hill. Look at the third house going up the hill to the right, the one with the altered gambrel roof partially blocked by an overgrown tree. This was originally a sea captain's home built in 1824, and Edward and Mary Scott lived at 17 Stony Hill throughout the '50s. At the time of his death, Mr. Scott had been head waiter at the Mohican Hotel for twenty-five years. A year later, Mrs. Scott sold their home to real estate investor Phyllis Hylton from Shapley Street. Mr. Hylton became a landlord once again and had another property to check up on.

These steps lead up to the Sebastian family home at 19 Stony Hill. Roy E. Sebastian was an elder of the Eastern Pequot Indians. He worked at Electric Boat as a welder and once ran for the board of education on the Republican ticket. An avid bow hunter, Sebastian loved the outdoors, and with redevelopment, the family moved on to Acorn Court. Two sons, Lawrence and Donald, went into the air force.

Stony Hill in winter. *Roger Dennis Collection, Lyman Allyn Museum.*

Stony Hill in spring, 1961. *George Oldershaw.*

Steps and fences, 1961. *George Oldershaw.*

View down Stony Hill, 1961. *George Oldershaw.*

217 Huntington Street, 1961. *George Oldershaw.*

Are you winded yet? There's more to come. We're looking back at 28 Stony Hill. On the right is the corner of 221 Huntington, so we're near the top. In trying to dig up some background on 28, I came across an issue of *The Junior Day*, a newspaper within a newspaper, where the contributors were under sixteen years old. Interesting, I thought. Marion Cluett, twelve, of 28 Stony Hill, wrote the following for the April 13, 1935 edition:

> *Don't Count Your Chickens*
>
> *Once there was a maiden who made her living by farming. There was one thing this maiden, called Molly, wanted, and that was a blue silken gown, trimmed in lace. So one day she bought a cow for a dollar—for cows were cheap those days. From the cow she got two gallons of milk each day and she planned to sell it and get a lot of money with which to buy the gown.*
>
> *But as it happened Molly's dog tipped over the milk pail and the cow ran away—and poor Molly—no gown she got.*

The Day reported on July 21, 1953, that Gail Marchand of 217 Huntington Street performed on *The Straw Hatters* television program on channel 5 at 8:30 p.m. Her second appearance this season, Gail also performed on Paul Whiteman's *Teen Agers* program. Why the fuss? Gail was a talented tap pupil of Virginia Latham of the Latham School of Dance (and voice) here in New London.

Chapter 10

MATHER COURT

We are in the backyard of 221 Huntington Street. Our photographer has caught Mary Sobczyk in her garden next to the garage at the end of Mather Court. The six houses on the east side of the street are owner-occupied one- and two-family homes. Linwood W. Bland Jr., president of the local NAACP chapter and author of *A View from the Sixties:*

Mary Sobczyk in her garden, 1961. *George Oldershaw.*

Exiting Mather Court, 1961. *George Oldershaw.*

The Black Experience in Southeastern Connecticut: A Memoir, lives in the fourth house from the left at 21 Mather Court. Like many other homeowners, Bland found the redevelopment award compensation less than adequate in securing another home elsewhere in the city. And yes, Cyril and Phyllis Hylton bought one of these homes, 29, in '59 for $6,000.

Mary Sobczyk's husband, Joseph, was now in a VA hospital. Starting in May 1962, she fell into a long illness that ended in death the next year. Her husband, Joseph, a World War I veteran in the Polish army and dock worker at the State Pier, followed his wife in '64.

We are walking south along Mather Court, named for Judge John P.C. Mather, who owned the land uphill from his ancestral home on Main Street. This quiet street ends at Richards Street, named for George Richards, who built a house on the corner with Main Street where Whaling City Ford is. The street was laid out in 1752 and was originally known as the highway to the burial place (Ye Antiest Burial Ground).

Hey, sailor!

Chapter 11

RICHARDS STREET

Through the power of this book, we have been magically transported to the bottom of Richards Street looking up from Main Street to Huntington. Here is the north side of the street. The small brick storefront on the right could be a great start-up location for a small business. It reminds me of a barbershop.

Here is the south side, with parallel parking and some snazzy cars. Let's continue up the street.

This two-family brick building at 22 Richards Street dates from 1854. The two Massad brothers, Solomon and David, live here with their families and have a small shirt-making plant in back. The two-story plant dates from 1948 and is made of brick over concrete block. The house on the above

Richards Street, north side, 1961. *George Oldershaw.*

Top: Richards Street, south side. *George Oldershaw.*

Middle: Massad Bros. Shirtmakers, 1961. *George Oldershaw.*

Bottom: Shirt factory (rear of property), 1961. *NLL.*

left is part of an apartment rental compound located in a former school on School House Lane. The mansard-roofed house on the above right is on Huntington Street.

Let's take one last glimpse down Richards Street toward the Massad Bros. home. It is interesting to note that they made burial shirts. Not T-shirts;

Top: View down south side of Richards from Huntington Street, 1961. *George Oldershaw.*

Bottom: 189 Huntington at Richards, 1961. *George Oldershaw.*

embroidered shirts you wore on your journey to the great beyond. Cool and comfortable, these shirts came with pockets for snacks and items to barter along the way, much like the Cuban guayabera. The brothers brought this practice over from Lebanon.

Here is another view from the top. We are looking north along Huntington Street with 189 just across Richards Street. According to the sign in the window, Mrs. Marino has furnished rooms for rent—but just for a year or so.

Chapter 12

HUNTINGTON STREET

We're walking south on the west side of Huntington toward St. James Episcopal Church, two doors down from Richards Street. On the left, the shingled house with the white trim is that of Mrs. Leybovitch at 179, Mrs. Hill at 175, Mrs. Snitkin at 171 and Mrs. Cuff with the mansard roof we've seen before, at 167. All are owner-occupied. All have an additional apartment or furnished rooms. This brings us to the northeast corner of Huntington and Hill Streets.

On the next corner stands the H.W. Reed realty office, "The Action Agency" at 165 Huntington. A crumpled "For Rent" sign is in the left-hand window. We are now in 1965, and demolition is already underway to the left on Hill Street. The double doors on the right are for the stairs going up to the apartment(s) above at 163. The right-side door has been left open. Tape and plastic cover one of the second-floor windows. The utilities have been shut off.

Next door at 161 is a locksmith shop, Miller being the name of the final tenant. The sign in the glass says "Open," but the passerby with bundles, dressed for warmth, seems to be looking in as if unconvinced. Its twin at 159 looks closed. The sign above says "Jason," and it's impossible to read the rest. Could this be the Jason soda canister service company? The stylized logo looks familiar. In the late '40s, people came here for homemade donuts and coffee. There was an oven in the back. The place was called the M&S Donut Shop. Smells good to me.

Top: The four Huntington homes on the way to Hill Street, 1961. *George Oldershaw.*

Middle: Reed Real Estate, 1964. *CONL.*

Bottom: Miner Grocery, 1964. *CONL.*

This grocery store at 157 Huntington came to my attention through Bebe Norman, who grew up with her sister Deborah Carter at 633 Main Street, not far from Al's Dug Out. She remembers visits to their grandparents on Shapley Street and trips to Mr. Miner's Grocery with allowance money. Snacks and sweets were kept at eye level. If they came up short, Mr. Miner would let it slide until their next visit, and always with a smile.

Frederick Miner lived with his family above at 155, an arrangement that had worked since before the First World War. His commute was up and down a flight of stairs, which must have helped keep a smile on his face, at least until 1965. He rented garage space behind his house.

Chapter 13

HILL STREET/SCHOOL HOUSE LANE

Let's double back to the top of Hill Street and walk down. It's easier that way.

This is 27 on the north side of Hill Street, abutting the west side of School House Lane. Note the red asphalt brick siding. The year is 1965, and the apartment house is empty and waiting for demolition. The neighboring houses to the left are gone such that you can see Bulkeley School. Cleveland Ford, a chipper at Electric Boat, lived here. Domingo Lozada, an employee at Ocean Beach Park, lived here as well with his wife, Ilena. And Mary McCants, a psychiatric aide at Norwich State Hospital, also called this home.

On the far right is the former Fifteenth District brick schoolhouse, which, starting in 1855, served 200 male "scholars" and 110 female. At some point before 1891, the school expanded with a frame L-shape addition in back, perhaps to reduce overcrowding or to provide staff with a convenient place to live.

The city closed and sold the school around 1900 to the Brainard and Armstrong Company on Union Street. The mill company had the two houses built, one on the north side and the other on the south, and used the school for storage. By 1907, the mill no longer needed the space and sold the property to a new owner who converted the school to rental housing. This is the south side of the school.

This is the north side with a six-room house. The address for the compound was 8 School House Lane regardless of which of the three buildings you lived in. All had indoor plumbing. The landlord had the former communal bathroom, or WC, converted into storage.

27 Hill Street, 1964. *CONL.*

8 School House Lane, south side, 1961. *George Oldershaw.*

Above: 12 School House Lane, north side, 1961. *NLL.*

Opposite, top: Exiting School House Lane back onto Hill, 1961. *George Oldershaw.*

Opposite, bottom: 23 Hill Street, 1961. *NLL.*

We're exiting School House Lane and rejoining Hill Street. The Colonial house directly in front with a chimney at either end is 28 Hill Street. Note the central entry door with sidelights. The back roof has a saltbox profile. The windows are six over nine. Underneath those asphalt shingles is clapboard siding. The year is 1961, and the house has already been empty for a couple of years. A small house stands in the backyard at 28½. A family remained there until demolition four years later. What we see on the right is the corner of 27.

Number 23 is on the north side of Hill Street, the east corner of School House Lane. This photo was taken in 1961. Willis Franklin, an elevator operator at the Mohican Hotel, lived in this house with his wife, Leonora, their son Willis Jr. and daughter-in-law Ann.

These homes are 9 and 7 on the north side of Hill Street looking down sometime in early '65. Note the interior doors on 9 nailed over the windows to keep intruders out. Hazel Wright, self-employed, lived here.

The neighboring house, 7, remained standing well into 1966. The homeowner, Adrian Boone, an adventurous spirit, had lived here for decades

with his wife, Minnie. They married in 1927 in Cristobal, Panama. Adrian, then twenty-seven, was from the Florida Panhandle, while Minnie, twenty-four, was a teacher from Jamaica. Later that year, the couple moved to New London (possibly due to a Navy connection) Adrian joined the Elks, Victory Lodge #1096, and Minnie jointed the Shiloh Baptist Church, singing in the choir and serving on the missionary board. They lived at 306 Main Street between Shapley and Hill. By '34, they had moved to 15 North Bank Street, where Adrian was running a private numbers lottery, and the police nabbed some of his employees. The judge fined him twenty-five dollars. Adrian made the papers two years later as a knife-wielding laborer out hunting to settle the score with a sailor who had punched him in the mouth at Shea's taproom on Green Street. A friend intervened, and the story goes no further. In the late '30s, Adrian worked for Louis Gonella in the billiards parlor below at 13 North Bank Street.

In August 1941, police raided the apartment above the pool hall at two o'clock in the morning and charged Adrian with running a "gambling resort." The buzzer warning system failed. Sergeant Frank Philopena and

9 and 7 Hill Street, 1964. *CONL/*

Patrolmen Dennis Murphy and Melvin Jetmore took $4.35 off the table as evidence and arrested Adrian and four "frequenters." Judge Sullivan fined Adrian $25 plus court costs and each of the four players $5. On New Year's Day 1943, there was a repeat performance at 7 Hill Street, where Adrian and Minnie had bought a home. Adrian was still working at the billiards parlor.

Two weeks later, *The Day* reported on a melee at the bus station lunch counter at 1:15 a.m. Three white sailors were knifed. Adrian admitted to pulling a knife in self-defense, but no more. Judge John T. Allen made the statement, "There should be no color distinction made in this case. I expect a thorough investigation by the police and every effort made to determine whether it was the Negroes or the white sailors who started the trouble." The case remains pending.

In either '43 or '44, Adrian and Minnie opened the Harlem Restaurant at 320 Main Street. While a display ad in *The Day* is customary for a grand opening, the Harlem Restaurant did well by word of mouth, be it on the street or at the sub base. The police reports might have deterred some, but the late-night dancing to a jukebox drew sailors and civilians alike. On June 5, 1944, the day before D-day, police stormed the restaurant and caught Adrian serving a drink to Palmerlee Tillman of School House Lane from behind the counter on a Sunday. Judge Boyer nolled the charge against Adrian, while Tillman took full responsibility for breaking the law. The judge fined the father of eight $100. On D-day, Adrian sold the Harlem to his wife, Minnie. On D-day plus one, Judge Boyer sentenced a sub base sailor to four months' jail time for the knife slashing of another at the restaurant.

Two years of relative quiet ensued before Adrian used a soda bottle in self-defense against another knife attack in the kitchen of the restaurant. Judge Richard Corkey had had enough and sentenced the suspect to twenty-five days in jail on Franklin Street. Another two years of peace came and went before police brought Adrian before the judge on charges of operating a house of ill fame at his home on Hill Street. Judge Wool nolled the charges for lack of evidence.

According to a certificate filed with the city clerk, Adrian submitted paperwork for the establishment of the Atlas Social Club of New London Incorporated with 7 Hill Street as the club address. Incorporators were Adrian and Minnie Boone, and the founding members were John G. Morgan of 12 Shapley Street (barman at Tiny's Heat Wave), Cyril Hylton of 45 Shapley Street and James Taylor of 18 Shapley Street. The stated goal was "to promote good fellowship among men of Negro extraction," according to *The Day* of October 10, 1949.

A short string of expensive events most likely led to the closing of the Harlem Restaurant in late 1951. Judge Gruskin fined the restaurant $100 for a liquor law violation after police discovered a customer with a beer in the kitchen on a Sunday. Minnie appeared in police court for selling liquor on Easter Sunday and later paid a $100 fine. The restaurant closed, and the sales went underground in the cellar of 7 Hill Street. With four police officers posing as customers, the "flourishing" trade came to a halt with a $150 fine and the promise of jail time for any recurrence.

Just in time for the summer season, a boat went missing—Adrian's. It was a fifteen-footer with a twenty-five-horsepower outboard. A flamingo pink paint job, shading to white at the bottom, should have made the boat easy to spot. Adrian kept the missing boat at Herman Marine Service, 178 Pequot Avenue. Perhaps if a reward were offered?

And then lastly, as if spurred on by change in the wind, Adrian went back to running a private lottery. Through a joint state and local effort, the police seized $1,482 in cash, an adding machine and policy slips in a search and seizure warrant served on the social club. Examination of the policy slips revealed bets of ten cents, fifty cents and one dollar. Bets went into a pool that determined the winning amount after the house (Adrian and six Hill, Shapley and Stony Hill residents) had taken its cut. Bets could be based on the closest correct answer to a question—such as the current balance in the U.S. Treasury or the final score in a local football game. In the end, Adrian Boone drew a fine of $100 for each of eight counts of policy playing and thirty days in jail, while his assistant and a close friend, Ellsworth Bell of Stony Hill, drew seven counts and sixty days in jail.

As I wrote earlier, the home of Adrian and Minnie Boone was the last to fall in the path of redevelopment. In 1971, as if to celebrate a ten-year anniversary, police busted another Adrian-Ellsworth numbers game, now playing on Manwaring Street. Last I heard, they posted bond and are still out. Minnie had the last laugh though—she lived to be one hundred.

This brings us to the bottom of Hill Street looking up in 1961. The street was named for Charles Hill, an early settler and town clerk who was granted the property between Main and Huntington Streets. Hill Street opened in 1752. For a while, locals referred to it as "Poverty Hill" due to the almshouse and modest means of the residents.

As you can see, the street has a grade. Part of the rationale behind the replacement of these side streets with terraced housing was to avoid these steep grades, replacing the vertical with the horizontal. Accidents happened, including two in 1961. An oil truck not far from the photographer had just finished making a delivery when the hand brake slipped and the heavy rear double tires gently rolled over the chocks. The driver and others watched as the truck picked up speed, took out a street sign and lodged itself in the corner of 324 Main Street, where storefront renovations had been underway.

The second "runaway" involved two boys, one six and the other seven, who released the hand brake on their father's car. After rolling thirty feet, the car slammed into a parked car, pushing it ten feet onto the sidewalk. Neither boy was hurt. By coincidence, that same year, I had climbed into my grandfather's Renault, intrigued by the shiny chrome levers and Scottish plaid upholstery, and managed to release the hand brake. The car started rolling down Farmington Avenue toward the woods waiting below. Had it not been for Joey Valentini bursting in on the passenger side and wrenching back up the hand brake lever, someone else would have written this book. Thanks, Joey!

This house (26 Hill Street) on the left, opposite School House Lane, has always intrigued me. The roof profile is that of a modest saltbox. It's covered with yellow asphalt shingles, and there are clapboards underneath. The 1901 Sanborn map marks the house as "old." With the help of Tom Schuch, local historian, and Jonathan Ayala, city clerk, I decided to dig a bit further.

Hill Street, south side, 1961. *George Oldershaw.*

According to land records, on March 3, 1803, Boston Freeman, a slave who worked the farm of John Miller in Quaker Hill, gained his emancipation through a Connecticut law that obliged the slaveholder—in this case John Miller—to cover all expenses incurred should a slave be "freed" and left in the care of the town. Rather than risk the cost of supporting Boston as he got older, John Miller let Boston go. By law, Boston had to be in good health and between the ages of twenty and forty. And so it was. A free man, Boston went to work in New London as an expressman—that is, he loaded and unloaded freight wagons, the means of transporting goods from one place to another. He was also a driver.

In 1810, Boston bought a lot on Hill Street through a mortgage with William Eldridge. Records show that he also bought property on Water Street through a mortgage with John Peck. In 1819, a house appears in subsequent land records pertaining to the lot. This house was 14 Hill Street. Other emancipated slaves lived in the house throughout the mid-1800s. One of them was Peter Hull, who acquired the house in marrying Martha Freeman, Boston's daughter.

Peter arrived in New London by way of a schooner he'd boarded with his father and his family in Florida during the 1840s. A free man whose trade was carpentry, Peter's father had worked for the English, saved his

26 Hill Street saltbox *(first house on left)*, 1961. *George Oldershaw.*

wages and bought the family's freedom and his own shortly before their departure from Florida. That journey instilled in Peter a love for the sea that would consume fifteen years of his life. When the lure of water started to wane, Peter remained home with Martha and worked as a coachman, a trade he'd learned while with his second master. (Peter's first master sold him after seeing the physical abuse suffered the young house servant at the hands of his wife.)

Martha passed at the age of 92 in 1898. Peter was 99. He spent the rest of his life going for strolls with his steady companion, a terrier that never left his side. On days when the weather cooperated, they went as far as the Parade or even the docks on the other side of the tracks. A sturdy cane helped steady Peter's step now that a disconnect was developing between his brain and his motor skills, a phenomenon he attributed to the frequent blows to the head delivered by his first master's wife. His hearing and understanding were good though, and wherever Peter happened to stop, people gladly spoke with him. He meant no harm to anyone. In the late afternoon when Peter returned home to 26 (née 14) Hill Street, his live-in niece was back from her day job and had a light dinner waiting for him. This arrangement lasted until June 1908. Peter fell ill and needed more attention until it was his turn to pass on July 16, 1908. At 109, Peter Hull was the longest-living resident in the state of Connecticut.

Chapter 14

SHAPLEY STREET

Our first look up Shapley Street confirms the steep climb ahead. On the left at 8 Shapley is the Sidney Mattress and Furniture manufacturing plant, with Sidney Sulman as president. In the early '20s, the company opened on the site of the former Ahavath Chesed Synagogue, which burned in early 1919, some say, due to arson. That was the opinion of society president Abraham Gordon, who ran grocery stores in the area before his family started the Yellow Front Package Store chain.

On an early fall day in 1933, Sidney Sulman's car slipped out of gear and started rolling down Shapley without parked cars to get in the way. The car crossed Main Street at more than a walking speed, narrowly missing traffic and pedestrians. It came to rest close to the New Haven tracks after taking out twenty feet of fence. After the initial reporting in *The Day* on September 23, no further news made the paper.

Sulman passed in '43, and his wife, Ida, took over with the help of two longtime associates. In '59, they sought a better location for their home center on Church Street and the bedding factory on Shapley. They found none and announced their closure in six months to cover contract obligations. A skeleton force remained for warranty service coverage until redevelopment bought the property in '65 for demolition.

We're looking across the street at what, until recently, was Miss Tyler's Beauty Shop at 11 Shapley Street. Tyler lived with a relative, Daisy Bright, and offered ironing and alterations services as well. She was also a near lifelong trustee of the Shiloh Baptist Church. On December 1, 1964, the two ladies sold their home and business to redevelopment for $8,000. A week later, Tyler resigned from the board of trustees at Shiloh.

Sidney Manufacturing, 1961. This was the site of New London's first synagogue, Ahavath Chesed, built in 1902 and destroyed by fire in 1918. *George Oldershaw.*

Miss Tyler's Beauty Salon and alterations, 1964. *CONL.*

The next house up along the north side of the street is Captain Adam Shapley's home at 15, built in 1761 on land that the captain's grandfather acquired through marriage. When New London's support of the privateers harassing the British fleet prompted General Arnold's burning of the ships, stores and warehouses, Captain Shapley commanded the American troops at Fort Trumbull. When it was evident that the fort was going to fall, Captain Shapley and his surviving men crossed in three boats over to Fort Griswold on Groton Heights and continued their defensive actions there (two boats made it). And there the commander nearly died. Captain Shapley returned to Shapley Street, his home untouched, due perhaps to its location away from the waterfront. There he languished for four months before dying.

In December 1913, Laura Anderson (O'Clair) worked as a spooler for Brainard and Armstrong on Union Street, where she was one of three hundred workers. Through contact with a relative living in Rhode Island, a rash developed on her skin. This was the second case of smallpox in the city, and it caused a stir. The mill sent Anderson home to 15 Shapley Street, and the health authorities kept her there under quarantine for four weeks. They vaccinated all those employed at the mill. All the neighbors got vaccinated. A month later, health officials lifted the quarantine. There were no new cases. It is unclear whether Anderson returned to the mill, but the following classified ad appeared in *The Day* on November 19, 1914: "Woman wants work by day or hour. Call 15 Shapley St., or address Elegant Worker, box 679."

And on March 7, 1919, the following: "Lost—Wednesday night, corner Bank and Reed and post office, black handbag containing rings and $8.81. Owner poor working woman. Please return to Laura Anderson, 15 Shapley street, first floor. Reward."

Mr. and Mrs. Marvin Hearn lived here as well in the '50s and early '60s. Mr. Hearn was a well-known and sought-after tenor and baritone who performed in church-related events at Shiloh. He worked as a butcher at the City Super Market opposite Beit Bros. on the southwest corner of Main and Masonic Streets. In an article supportive of civil rights, the paper focused on Hearn's progression from stock clerk to butcher and customer service as a sign of slow but steady change in societal attitudes and norms. In 1957, this was news. On Valentine's Day 1958, Hearn and his wife, Frances, formed the Non-Partisan Social Club. Initial members included Catherine Baldwin, Edith Reyes and Robert Reyes.

The last family to call 15 Shapley Street home were the Bordens. Edward Borden worked as a chef at the Lighthouse Inn. After the landlord, McKinley Jones, sold the property to redevelopment, the wife and children started packing for the move to Groton. While they were away during one of their trips across the river, a group of fifteen children, ages five to fourteen, broke into the house and ripped open the packed bags and boxes, strewing the family's belongings throughout the house. They also damaged lighting fixtures and water pipes, making the place no longer livable. The police rounded up the children and planned on investigating, reported *The Day* on November 28, 1964.

This may be a stretch, but there are parallels here with the flattened landscapes of Berlin and Warsaw during the last days of war and the first days of peace in 1945. Months and months of demolition had passed, homes and businesses being smashed without, in the eyes of a child, any meaningful consequence. No police stepped in. The neighbors and their friends were gone or leaving, the adult eyes on the street no longer watching. Some children were in many ways left on their own, like the stranded middle-class boys in William Golding's *Lord of the Flies*. This surreal environment of social disintegration in no way justifies the feral behavior of these children, yet this thought must have gone through the back of their heads—they're leaving, we're not.

What's your take on this?

Looking down Shapley toward Main, Captain Adam Shapley saltbox on left, 1964. *CONL.*

The Shapley princesses, north side, 1964. *CONL.*

These houses climbing the north side of the street—19, 23, 25 and 31—I call the Shapley princesses. They are the bay-windowed "cottages" with gingerbread trim and dormered mansard roofs, nieces to the Queen Annes of San Francisco. The Simon family from Lebanon live in 19 and 23. The Reverend Donald Davis and his wife, Anna, live in 25.

On January 7, 1957, *The Day* ran a story on Kaleel and Nazera Simon celebrating their fiftieth wedding anniversary at Mabrey's by Ocean Beach. The couple met in romantic Willimantic. Mr. Simon had retired from Rossie Velvet and Electric Boat and was a cousin to Reverend Simon Hage, pastor of St. Ann's on Connecticut Avenue (since moved to Waterford). One daughter, Margaret Lukas, lived next door at 19.

John and Mary Lasky lived at 31 Shapley, shown here boarded up and awaiting demolition in 1965. Mr. Lasky was active in the American Legion and the Sea Scouts out of the sub base. On October 31, 1947, *The Day* reported on his stepson, Sergeant Major Joseph Thomas Lasky of the marine corps, coming home from a 1944 ultimate sacrifice visit to Saipan in the Pacific to engage the Japanese. Hundreds showed up to honor him at Union Station as the train from New York slowly pulled in. Mr. and Mrs. Lasky waited in their car.

Top: Kaleel and Nazera Simon, 1957. *From* The Day.

Middle: The Lasky house, east side, 1964. *CONL*.

Bottom: The Lasky house, west side. *CONL*.

The shingled two-story gambrel house at 26 Shapley has been in the Glassberg family since 1919. The family lived on the second floor while renting out the five-room apartment on the first and furnished rooms in the attic. As with many other boardinghouses, the Glassbergs had their share of drama from time to time, as evidenced by police reports in the paper. They remained until redevelopment. Margo Santos lived her New London High School years here and, after working a summer as a nurse's aide, entered the Lawrence School of Nursing at L&M for what promised to be a rewarding career helping others.

The frame duplex next door at 30 was the home of Mr. L'Ouverture "Luke" Harris and his wife, Mrs. Jeanette Coleman Harris. Originally from Virginia, this was their first home. Jeanette was a housekeeper and former matron of the Electra Chapter of the Order of the Eastern Star. She also belonged to the Daughters of Isis. At the age of fifty, many felt, especially Luke, that she had passed too early after a month of illness.

Luke played for the semi-pro New London Colored Giants in the '30s as a popular catcher. He stayed with the team as they became the New London

The Glassberg house, 1961. *George Oldershaw.*

Whalers. Luke started working as a bellhop at the Mohican Hotel before spending twenty-three years as an Electric Boat carpenter. Along with his friend Henry Fulford, who had also harvested coal from the New Haven tracks, Luke was part of the Yergan and Hackley Dramatic Clubs, putting on such performances as *The Wayfarers* and *Bubbles*.

In late '64, Luke sold his home to redevelopment and, like many homeowners, found the awarded compensation inadequate in trying to buy another home elsewhere. Luke moved to Shaw Street and retired from Electric Boat. A social butterfly, he enjoyed being out twice a day greeting children and parents as a school crossing guard. Luke was a founding member of the New London branch of the NAACP, a member of the Victory Lodge of Elks, a past potentate of the Imperial Council AEAONMS, Inc. of the Arabic Temple and the business advisor to the Imperial Carib Club of Phyllis and Cyril Hylton, neighbors up the street. Both Luke and Jean spent much time at the social events hosted by the Hempstead Hall. Luke passed on the tenth anniversary of Jean's departure.

Top: South side, upper Shapley. The Harris house is third on the right, 1961. *George Oldershaw.*

Bottom: Luke and Jeanette Harris, circa 1960. *Courtesy Jean Jordan.*

Shapley Street, 1965. *Roger Dennis Collection, Lyman Allyn Museum.*

We will leave off on Shapley Street with a watercolor portrait from artist Roger Dennis, whose work is in the collection of the Lyman Allyn Art Museum here in New London. You may recognize or imagine the scene he has depicted.

This brings us to the upper corner of Shapley and Huntington Streets, a historically significant location. In the 1840s, there were two houses—51 and 45–43 Shapley—along with a stable behind 51. The three buildings belonged to the Anderson couple, Celinda Harris and William, both descendants of freed slaves. They converted the stable into Good Samaritan Hall, where members of abolitionist groups came to speak and a school for Black children was established under the direction of Olive Harris Olney.

Fast-forward to the 1930s. Both the house at 51 and the Good Samaritan Hall were empty and had fallen into disrepair. The city ordered both buildings demolished. Sam Gruskin, a Shapley Street neighbor, built a garage and gas station on the site in 1937. At that time, William and Estella Gambles were living at 45–43, where they ran a rec hall and tearoom. A chief steward for the Coast Guard, Mr. Gambles also opened a school for catering at the same location. The couple made rooms for tourists also available, as both

Cyril and Phyllis Hylton, 1960. *From* The Day.

the Crocker House and the Mohican Hotel refused service to Black guests, according to Tom Schuch's website "Black Heritage Trail."

In the mid-'40s, 45–43 saw new stewards come into town and move in. The Jamaican couple Cyril and Phyllis Hylton opened the Imperial Restaurant on Main Street in 1943. They became members of the Shiloh Baptist community and founded the Imperial Carib Club, which through fun-centered fundraisers helped the church's building fund as well as the residents of the city-run Hillside Home through the club's Christmas parties. A staunch Democrat, "Ma" Hylton hosted a "stop for coffee" visit in the Fourth Ward for congressional candidate Douglas J. Bennet of Lyme at her home. The fifteen-minute visit followed another at the R&J Underwear Company at 54 Coit Street. Firm believers in accumulating wealth for their charitable interests through real estate investment, the Hyltons had amassed sixteen properties in the Main Street area. Redevelopment took them all, including their own home at 45 Shapley Street.

Chapter 15

FEDERAL STREET

Of all the streets consumed by redevelopment, this stretch of Federal Street from Main to Huntington was the most elegant. On the south side was the American Methodist Episcopalian (AME) Church, built in 1856. After the Ahavath Chesed Synagogue burned in 1919, the society made its new home here, with Rabbi David Traub and family living next door at 50 Federal around 1960. As the suburbanization of our car culture prompted a further exodus of neighborhood members, it was decided to abandon the synagogue in favor of a new one built on Montauk Avenue. Thanks to the efforts and vision of attorney Francis McGuire, the Acorn Barnes home up the street at 68 Federal was rehabbed and saved at the corner of Meridian and Federal. And though not on the redevelopment table, the red brick parish house for St. James Episcopal Church was lost to a parking lot on the other corner, its purpose replaced by the modern Seabury Center.

We are starting at the corner of Federal and Main Streets, looking across the manicured lawn of the B.P. Learned House. Note the granite block knee-wall and the wrought-iron fence, the grace of the ornamental streetlamp. Below is a police callbox, around the corner a red fire alarm box. On the far side of Federal is the Polish American Club (brick) at 206 Main and a rooming house on the right at 30 Federal.

One living arrangement that New London lost to a large degree was the rooming house. For a modest cost, you got a furnished room with either meals served in a dining room or kitchen privileges. You could stay by the week, month or year. And while there was drama at times, there was also love, in the spring and in the summer. Before the digital age in which we now live, there was the newspaper and, in some places, there still is. *The Day* carried "Intentions of Marriage" as brief announcements. In the spring of 1940, Harold Steves and Marie Chagnon, both residing at 30 Federal Street, had gone to the city clerk's office to formalize their plans. In the summer of 1961, boardinghouse sweethearts George Redding, a welder, and Delores Turner, a waitress, did the same.

We are staying on the north side of Federal Street and looking up toward Huntington. Police headquarters is to our left out of the picture, and the Eagles Club and Home is opposite at 114 Union Street. It's a Sunday morning in 1961; three children are walking toward us, and there's a little church traffic up by St. James. On the left behind a large leafy tree, we can see the decorative brickwork of the old AME church, now the Ahavath Chesed Synagogue.

Top: Federal Street at Main, with the Polish Club in the background, 1961. *George Oldershaw.*

Bottom: View up Federal Street, with the Ahavath Chesed Synagogue (former Methodist Episcopalian Church) visible above the large tree on the left, 1961. *George Oldershaw.*

Above: 37 Federal Street, 1961. *George Oldershaw.*

Left: Villa at 45 Federal Street, 1961. *George Oldershaw.*

From left to right, we are looking at the corner of 41, 37 and the extension of the Learned House on another day. Number 37 has an apartment on each floor, judging by the three mailboxes and the back fire escape. Those mansard dormers are stunning and must have provided a good view to the east of the harbor. My guess is that this was a single-family home in the beginning.

The children are back taking a break to play, perhaps in front of their home, either 45 or 41 Federal. Similar in design to the former Lawrence villa, now the Learned House, 45 was home to the Robert Tate family for most of the 1900s, and in the last years, Navy families stayed in the two apartments.

On July 13, 1898, when this villa was the home of Mr. S.D. Leadbeater, *The Day* reported the loss of Baby, a trick dog known for killing record numbers of rats. Baby was four years old and weighed just two and one-half pounds. At the time of her death, Baby had recently won first prize at the New Jersey State Fair and had plans to compete in the Wyoming County (Pennsylvania) fair in September.

The Henkle Home at 51 Federal Street is another variation of the villas popular in the mid-1800s. Since 1903, there has always been a Henkle in the house. Dr. Emanuel Henkle, a prominent physician and surgeon, moved his family and practice here from Tilley Street. He was a founder of Lawrence and Memorial Hospitals and over the course of his career delivered 6,600 babies, two being his sons: Robert, a doctor, and Edward, New London's city manager until 1963. Dr. Henkle also served on the board of education and, as a young man, played the violin.

Top: Henkle House, 1964. *CONL.*

Bottom: Winter at the Henkle House, 1966. *George Oldershaw.*

Top, left: Summer at the Henkle House, 1966. Note the boarded-up windows on either side. *George Oldershaw.*

Top, right: Interior front of the Henkle House as it is coming down, 1966. Note the door profile. Ahavath Chesed is visible above. *George Oldershaw.*

Bottom: Twilight at the Henkle House, 1966. *George Oldershaw.*

The main entrance to the Henkle House was on Federal Street. Over the last ten years, the house was rented out, generally to Navy families.

The next home is the Mumford House at 65 Federal Street, built by one of the most prominent families in colonial New London. Like many others, the Mumford family profited from trade with the West Indies, notably Barbados and Nevis. As mentioned before, the trade largely involved the shipment of horses and iron goods such as tools and cookware in return for rum, sugar, molasses and African slaves, a market that remained legal until 1848, just months after the Douglass talks at Dart Hall. The home was later the first parish house for the St. James Episcopal Church diagonally across the street.

Top: Captain Giles Mumford House (circa 1792), 1961. *George Oldershaw.*

Middle: Alderson-Prentis Funeral Home, 1964. *CONL.*

Bottom: Carriageway at Alderson-Prentis, 1961. *George Oldershaw.*

Top: Carriage house, rear of property, 1961. The upper floor was used for coffin storage. The back of this brick "castle" ran along Shapley Street, opposite the Hylton house. *George Oldershaw.*

Bottom: Alderson-Prentis coming down, one bucketful at a time, 1966. *George Oldershaw.*

Next, we are looking at the Alderson-Prentis Funeral Home at 75 Federal Street. Its carriageway speaks of a certain dignity afforded when paying final respects, be it in a carriage or a car. Meridian Street is on the other side.

Our last stop on Federal Street is the Labensky House at 85. Alfred Labensky was a Bulkeley boy, class of 1908, with a bright future. An active hunter and fisherman, the young man was interested in electricity and worked as an X-ray lab technician before entering college. In 1928, the young doctor moved his practice and bride, Dorothy Himberg, a registered nurse, to 85 Federal Street. Dr. Labensky would go on to work as chief of staff at the Lawrence and Memorial Hospital for twenty-one years. (And yes, his neighbor Dr. Henkle came to my mind as well.) In 1958, Dr. Labensky passed on, having survived his wife. His funeral took place next door at Alderson-Prentis.

Top: 85 Federal Street, 1964. *CONL*.

Bottom: Demolition of 85 Federal Street, 1966. *George Oldershaw*.

In 1965, the Labensky House was empty and a little boy approached to investigate. The loss of this building would leave a void at that corner for at least twenty years until a senior high-rise took charge behind a chain-link fence.

Chapter 16

MERIDIAN STREET

This is the short residential block that will bring us to Church Street, now called Governor Winthrop Boulevard. We are looking at the east side toward the YMCA and the Mohican Hotel. The barn-like structure in the left foreground with the garage doors and vertical Goodrich Tire sign is intriguing. Today is trash day. Tuesday and Fridays were our trash days. What about you?

This is the west side of Meridian Street. Again, we are strolling with George Oldershaw on a Sunday morning in 1961. The white-painted three-story brick building is worth a closer look.

This close-up shot of 46 Meridian Street dates from 1965. Note the hanging sign for attorneys McGarry, Prince, Fox, and McGarry in front is gone, and someone has removed the two bronze plaques from the wall. Christopher Associates, owners of the building, protested the demolition of their building through their lawyers on the first floor at an early public hearing. The hearing also covered the possibility of moving the circa 1835 Federal-style building next to the Barnes House renovated in '56 by the Francis McGuire law firm. The discussion doesn't seem to have gone any further as to the logistics and cost of the move. House movers use rollers and/or tractors. A three-story brick building moving across an already cleared pathway should have been possible. The mindset at the time, however, was for demolition. The federal funding made no provisions for moving, and so the bureaucrats didn't budge.

Meridian Street, east side, Mohican Hotel in background, 1961. *George Oldershaw.*

Meridian Street, west side, 1961. *George Oldershaw.*

During the various phases of the project, redevelopment used different buildings in a leapfrog-like manner as field offices, and such was the case in 1965. In December, a person or persons broke in, ransacked the office on the first floor and set a fire. The second- and third-floor apartments were vacant and spared any damage other than smoke and water. One

Opposite: 46 Meridian Street before arson fire, 1965. *CONL.*

Right: 46 Meridian Street (circa 1840s), 1961. *George Oldershaw.*

item was missing: a new typewriter. Police found it, interestingly enough, on the front seat of a car parked on Shapley Street. Police also found no sign of a forced entry.

The matter was dropped. Redevelopment relocated the following Monday to another doomed building, this time 31 Church Street, around the corner. Although the fire had been confined to the first floor, the city condemned the building as a total loss. Plans remained in place to demolish the historic structure for future development and reuse—as a parking lot.

Chapter 17

CHURCH STREET (GOVERNOR WINTHROP BOULEVARD)

We've walked to the end of this block on Meridian and have turned right up Church toward Huntington and the A&P. Church Street has two travel lanes with parking on either side.

The home of the YWCA is on the right at the top, 93 Huntington, with an entrance shown at 73 Church Street. In 1919, the "Y" moved here from the former Lawrence villa, later known as the Learned House. The chimney alone is a masterpiece of brickwork, but the redevelopment rationale behind demolition was to widen Church Street to boulevard proportions.

Another gem, this one at 63 Church Street, is the circa 1801 Learned-Bunner House, where attorneys Hirsch, Washton (former police court judge and Democratic Town Committee chair), Vogt and Traystman ran their practices. Again, redevelopment wanted all structures down for street widening. To her credit, Mildred C. Greene of 33 Shirley Lane outlined in a letter to *The Day* how the building matches redevelopment's own criteria for preservation. Both attorneys Washton and Vogt had also expressed interest in having the house moved. It is interesting to note that an apartment was listed for rent in the floors above later that summer. In the end, the moving plan never gained traction or the right support.

We are back by the northeast corner of Church and Meridian Streets, and it's a full deck. The house with the turret and witch's cap is 33 Meridian Street, home to a Navy family with children. Gates and Beckwith, a paint, wallpaper and home decorating standby for New London since it had been Hobron & Root in 1901, is front and center. Under the leadership of Curtis

YWCA, corner of Church and Huntington Streets, 1961. *George Oldershaw.*

Brunner House (circa 1800), 1961. *George Oldershaw.*

Gates and Beckwith, 1961. *George Oldershaw.*

Hobron & Root, circa 1910. *Courtesy Shirley Beckwith.*

New London home decorators' convention, 1926, hosted by Gates and Beckwith. *Courtesy Shirley Beckwith.*

Gates and Howard Beckwith, the firm hosted a home décor convention in 1926 that brought many dealers and customers to town for the first time. The event was a huge marketing success.

The store moved south of Hodges Square to 297 Williams Street in '65, only to be impacted later on by the highway connections serving a planned

Top: Gates and Beckwith have moved, 1964. *George Oldershaw.*

Bottom: Remington Rand office machines, 1965. *CONL.*

second span across the Thames River in '71. The western half of Hodges Square would disappear, and the new store location above Fremont Street would be buried under the Route 32 expressway connecting with downtown.

The offices and showroom spaces of the Remington Rand Division of Sperry Rand were at 39–41 Church Street. The company made office machinery and left in '64. Frances Baldini was the manager. Note through the breezeway on the left that the Gates and Beckwith building is already gone. We are in 1965, and the juggernaut of redevelopment is getting a second wind.

Chapter 18

UNION STREET

Our last street on this tour. The rear section of the nave to the First Congregational Church stands to the left across from the corner of Masonic Street and the post office. The two-story brick structure at 66 Union Street is the Konomoc Aerial Ladder Company. Joe DiMaggio remembers being the tiller man steering the tail end of the ladder and backing up on such narrow street entries as Mather Court and the constant "jump on and pray" routine whenever a call came in. They wore light gray work uniforms and had binoculars at the ready whenever the subject of architecture at the Mohican Hotel came up. Joe recalls sharing a respirator and hoping the nearest hydrant hadn't frozen up, that the freezing rain, which had no deterrent effect on the fire, would let up. This required a steady faith in miracles, wherever and whenever. As with the leapfrog movements already mentioned, redevelopment used the vacant ladder company as a temporary field office before it came down.

The large brick building to the right, filling in the rest of the block to Church Street, is the former Brainard and Armstrong mill built in 1890. In 1945, this building went up for sale by auction. The City of New London planned on a winning bid of $50,000 in order to carry out plans for the mill's demolition (do you see a pattern here?) and replacement with a new municipal building that would consolidate city departments and provide parking.

Max Beit (Beit Bros. Market) of Union Realty secured the purchase of 82 Union Street with a bid of $250,000 and had the vision to update the mill

Above: Konomoc Aerial Ladder Company, former Brainard & Armstrong silk mill, 1961. *George Oldershaw.*

Opposite: Page from Jay-Fro catalogue, 1963. *Courtesy Elaine Maynard Adams.*

and section it off for manufacturing tenants, thus drawing in startups looking for lower-rent raw industrial space. The idea, planning and investment worked. Following is a list of the eight tenants using the mill at the time of the redevelopment referendum in April 1962:

1. Thomas B. Faria Corporation (tachometers) (Denison Avenue)
2. Tunxis Sportswear Manufacturing The Rabitz Family (Mansfield Road)
3. Cameo Manufacturing (women's dresses)
4. New London Instrument Company
5. Jay-Fro Athletic Supply John and Sherry Kroll
6. Sullivan Printing
7. Bedge Brassiere Manufacturing
8. Monroe Calculating Machine Co.

John Kroll was a physical education teacher in New London Public Schools before starting Jay-Fro with his wife, Sherry. Tom Faria started

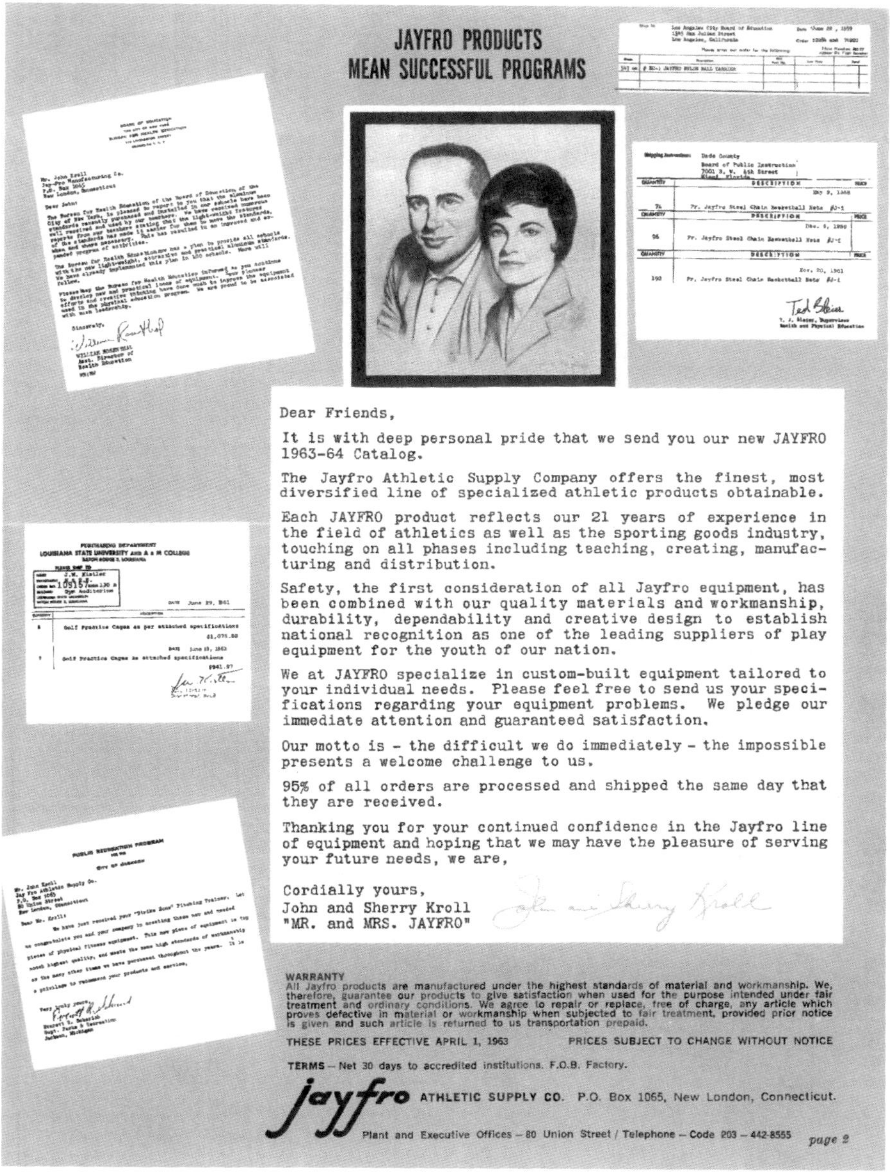

JAYFRO PRODUCTS
MEAN SUCCESSFUL PROGRAMS

Dear Friends,

It is with deep personal pride that we send you our new JAYFRO 1963-64 Catalog.

The Jayfro Athletic Supply Company offers the finest, most diversified line of specialized athletic products obtainable.

Each JAYFRO product reflects our 21 years of experience in the field of athletics as well as the sporting goods industry, touching on all phases including teaching, creating, manufacturing and distribution.

Safety, the first consideration of all Jayfro equipment, has been combined with our quality materials and workmanship, durability, dependability and creative design to establish national recognition as one of the leading suppliers of play equipment for the youth of our nation.

We at JAYFRO specialize in custom-built equipment tailored to your individual needs. Please feel free to send us your specifications regarding your equipment problems. We pledge our immediate attention and guaranteed satisfaction.

Our motto is - the difficult we do immediately - the impossible presents a welcome challenge to us.

95% of all orders are processed and shipped the same day that they are received.

Thanking you for your continued confidence in the Jayfro line of equipment and hoping that we may have the pleasure of serving your future needs, we are,

Cordially yours,
John and Sherry Kroll
"MR. and MRS. JAYFRO"

WARRANTY
All Jayfro products are manufactured under the highest standards of material and workmanship. We, therefore, guarantee our products to give satisfaction when used for the purpose intended under fair treatment and ordinary conditions. We agree to repair or replace, free of charge, any article which proves defective in material or workmanship when subjected to fair treatment, provided prior notice is given and such article is returned to us transportation prepaid.

THESE PRICES EFFECTIVE APRIL 1, 1963 PRICES SUBJECT TO CHANGE WITHOUT NOTICE

TERMS – Net 30 days to accredited institutions. F.O.B. Factory.

jayfro ATHLETIC SUPPLY CO. P.O. Box 1065, New London, Connecticut.
Plant and Executive Offices – 80 Union Street / Telephone – Code 203 – 442-8555

page 2

working on early vacuum tube battery radios while growing up on Denison Avenue. Sidney Ravitz of Tunxis Sportswear learned the clothing market from a relative in Brooklyn before coming to New London. Dr. Dale Pollack, president and one of three founding partners of the New London Instrument Company, would later work with an associated electronics institute in Rehovoth, Israel, on a first-of-its-kind computer.

Brainard and Armstrong stair tower, interior courtyard. *George Oldershaw.*

Brainard and Armstrong demolition for planned parking garage. *George Oldershaw.*

Parish house, custodian's house (circa 1800), 1961. *George Oldershaw.*

The Bedge Brassiere Manufacturing Company was the last tenant to leave the Beit Mill before demolition in 1969. The company had two hundred employees and was controlled by a larger parent. Manager Otto Tonti was working with redevelopment on a new location as a 550-car parking garage was planned for the site. By summer, a new location for the company had been found at 35 Pequot Avenue, and the last mill tenant left. On September 11, 1969, seventy-nine years of manufacturing and innovation at 82 Union Street came to an end.

On the southeast corner of Church and Union stands the Parish House of the First Congregational Church at 79 Union Street. The gambrel-roofed house on the right is 75, thought to be the home of the church caretaker's family. Both are now a parking and turning lot for post office vehicles.

This unusual house on the northeast corner at 91 Union Street was the home of George and Mary Pratt of Aberdeen, Scotland. Mr. Pratt worked for the city as a stonecutter, a trade his son George Jr. took with him to Barre, Vermont.

A more recent resident would be Mary Ferrigno, a secretary at Pfizer in Groton. On New Year's Eve 1959, she found herself in the middle of a revolution in Havana, Cuba. The U.S.-backed President Fulgencio Baptista was flying out to Miami, and el comandante en jefe Fidel "el Querido"

"Turret House," 1961. *George Oldershaw.*

Union Street, heading back to Federal, 1961. *George Oldershaw.*

Castro was marching in. Mary and her cruise ship group made it back from an empty nightclub to the hotel, where they were searched for guns and cameras, and then from the hotel back to their ship. The ducking at rifle shots was nerve wracking, she remembered in *The Day* on January 7, 1959, but the happiness of the people was highly contagious.

And this is the quiet residential west side of Union Street taking us from Church back to Federal Street. We are looking at the northwest corner. The first house on the left, 92, is the home of the Gorra family, the same who own and manage the fruit market at 20 Main Street. On the east side of the block at the end stands police headquarters, the former Stanton School. This building at 111 Union Street now serves various city departments, including public works and the building department. Walking along the right side toward the back, you'll find a marker as part of the Black Heritage Trail. At this site, Ichabod Pease, a freed slave and parishioner at St. James, opened a school for Black children at the age of eighty-one and ran the school from 1837 to 1839, at which point segregation ended in the New London public schools.

Chapter 19

THE BLUE (CHECKER) CAB CO.

And finally, yes, a cabbie's perspective on the universe about to be lost. A young man on a summer job, a future writer, a reporter with a flair for people, for rubbing elbows, taking mental notes and squirreling them away for immediate recall at the right time in the right place. By way of an epilogue, we are in the summer of '65, hands tight on the wheel of a boxy blue-and-white tank riding on four balding tires, brakes slipping, the slight smell of vomit rising from the back seat, cigarette butts on the floor and a license plate: 022.

"22, 22…pick up at First National."

Loading the bags, all seven of them, one by one.

"You're going the wrong way! You new around here? I ain't paying you for this. No! Take a left here, I don't care it's one-way!"

Unloading. One by one. On the steps. Young men hanging out—staring, faces blank of intention. Her nephews? Grandchildren? The coffee can stashed under the front seat—key still in the ignition. Damn. Head on a swivel, eyes in back.

"No! Inside! You expect me to carry them upstairs by myself?" She clutches her small cloth purse.

Steep, narrow, rickety stairs—loose handrails or missing, broken. Paper bags, not doubled, slip, fall, break open.

A quick in and out like NASA, as my father would say. Claustrophobic smells of failed meals, dollar-a-bottle perfume, layers of body odor, windows nailed or painted shut against the outside, at all times, rain or shine.

Finally back…an eleven-cent tip. They're gone. Cab still there. Key still there. Chock full o'Nuts can still there. My wad untouched.

"Take the keys. Don't let a good boy go bad." Public service announcement.

"22, 22…pick up, 607 Main Street."

I slow down and look at the house numbers—531…549…563…571. Honking, there's a line of cars behind me. I pull over, hear an unkind remark whiz by me and look down the street to where 607 Main should be. There's a burly man in a white T-shirt leaning into a small short woman with wild hair and sunglasses. There's stuff all over the sidewalk—broken bags of clothes, boxes of shoes and toys, piles of blankets and sheets, a damaged end table flipped over, a lamp with a smashed-in shade. The woman screams something. The guy slaps her hard, turns and goes back into the apartment house. The windows are open, a breeze lifts what's left of some curtains. The place looks slumped, exhausted. I have never noticed it before. The woman picks her sunglasses off the ground and turns. She's looking at me. She waves or hails me, just like Fifth Avenue.

You're on, champ.

Seagulls screeching overhead. Gray sky, darkening clouds. You can smell Winthrop Cove behind these buildings—low tide, organic rot, decay, slime. A seagull drops one on the windshield. It starts to rain. I forgot to check the wipers this morning.

The woman waves again, this time more emphatically. I'm the rescue pilot, she's the castaway.

"What took you so long? I called over an hour ago."

I motion to the stuff strewn on the sidewalk and in the gutter.

"I'm not a moving van, Miss."

Then I hear him, a boy of four or five, sitting behind one of the larger clothes bags, crying. He has on a dirty T-shirt and is missing one sneaker and a sock. Checker cabs are roomy. Great for furniture. Great for moving furniture. The woman, now a mother, gets almost everything into the back. She's had practice. A mattress is propped against the wall by the mailboxes.

"You got rope?"

We waltz the mattress over to the cab and push it so that it droops over the "vacant" light and roof. The stuff is now wet. The kid is still crying. Sitting in his mother's lap on the front side doesn't seem to be having any effect.

"So, where to?"

The mother looks down the street, makes a vague gesture with her hand.

"Oh…down that way. Hill Street."

The inside of me moans. With one hand on the wheel, the other out holding my side of the mattress, we wait for traffic and make a U-turn, just clearing a truck parked on the other side. The wipers don't work. We turn right up Hill and start climbing, the mattress half on, half off. The rain stops as we reach a house near the top. The kid is still crying. I reach into my shirt pocket for a roll of Lifesavers, snap one off the roll, look at the boy and say, "Cherry."

The mother snatches it, shoves it in his mouth, and there's quiet. The street is empty. A couple of houses have already been demolished. Three dogs, perhaps left behind, study us from across the street. We unload the cab. I notice a large open porch on the second floor. The front door below is open, the hardware missing.

"Glad to be out of that dump."

I nod and stand still by the cab, signaling it's time to go.

The mother's mouth remains half open. She's holding her sunglasses and wipes the hair from her face. I notice that she is looking at me for the first time.

"Thank you. Now how do you want to be paid?"

I feel a blush coming on, and it's annoying.

"Cash is king. The meter says a dollar thirty-seven."

She reaches into her jeans and pulls out two crumpled one-dollar bills. No eye contact. The boy is off to the side staring at his next home, then looking at the dogs across the street.

There's a squeal from what we call the bitch box.

"22… 22…"

"Gotta go, we're busy."

The mother has a bag and is heading for the front door.

"Good luck."

No answer. I turn for the cab and, on impulse, leave the roll of Lifesavers on the end table.

Two days later, I get a call late in the afternoon, just before the end of my shift.

"22…22…pickup, 38 Hill Street."

I don't recognize the address until I'm practically in front of the place. The front door is open. I hear a door slam on the second floor. She rushes from the house to the rear door of the cab as if possessed. A flowing, orange print dress with a black satin scarf, her nails done, hair drawn back, face restored—mother is radiant.

Blue Checker Cabs waiting for fares on the Parade, 1961. *George Oldershaw.*

She sits in back, pulls a mirror out of nowhere and checks herself. Absorbed for the moment, nothing happens. I wait and, after a moment, pull down the lever.

Mother addresses the back of my head, turned slightly toward her.

"Driver, take me to Skrigan's!"

EPILOGUE

Through this book, I have attempted to provide you, the reader, with a glimpse of the people and places that existed within the Main Street neighborhoods before and during the redevelopment period of the 1960s.

Celia Cruz sings, *La vida es un carnaval.* In many ways, in better days, Main Street and North Bank Street were the show, the side streets and alleys the popcorn section. The Borax twenty-mule team was in town. On Saturday mornings, there was the children's talent show at the Victory Theater on the Parade. Coleman Bros. set up in Waterford. Ocean Beach offered candied apples, the Bullet, a train ride and the landmark clock tower. Cheap thrills in a simpler time. Something for everyone.

In the '60s, we started losing that. Color television kept us home most evenings, and later the car took us to the mall or casino. This freedom and desire to move quickly required space, lots of it. And so with each building that came down, a home or business was erased, an entry-level admission to what New London had to offer or, at the very least, a holding pattern for those stuck in neutral. The boardinghouses, rooms for rent, laundromats, cheap restaurants, small starter storefronts, corner groceries and social clubs would not be replaced.

Perhaps it's time to rethink what our parents and their parents so quickly discarded.

BIBLIOGRAPHY

Anderson, Martin. *The Federal Bulldozer.* MIT Press, 1964.

Blanchard, Bob. *Lost Burlington, Vermont.* The History Press, 2023.

Bland, Linwood T. *A View from the 60's: The Black Experience in Southeastern Connecticut.* New London County Historical Society, 2001.

Caulkins, Frances M. *History of New London, Connecticut.* H.D. Utley, 1895.

The Day archives. newspapers.com.

Jacobs, Jane. *The Death and Life of Great American Cities.* Vintage Books, 1961.

Kanzler, Carmelina Como. *New London: A History of Its People.* City of New London, 1996.

Keating, Sergeant Lawrence, Sr., and Catherine Keating. *New London Police Department.* Arcadia Publishing, 2019.

Noyes, Gertrude E. *The Savings Bank of New London at 150.* Savings Bank of New London, 1977.

Ruddy, John. *Reinventing New London.* Arcadia Publishing, 2000.

Samul, Tara. *New London Firefighting.* Arcadia Publishing, 2006.

Vallye, Anna. *Urban Renewal and Highway Construction in New London, 1941–1975.* New London County Historical Society, 2021.

ABOUT THE AUTHOR

Perhaps this interest in lost places began with a road trip to California our family made in pre-interstate 1961. I was five and remember the crumbling, abandoned structures out west dotting the federal highway. They intrigued me more than a pool and swing set. I begged my father to pull over and let us explore. My fantasy was to move in, rough it like the early pioneers and bring the house or store back to life, quickly, as if by magic. While we didn't stop, my father did buy me a hammer for my birthday, an improvement over the rocks I'd used for pounding and straightening the nails needed in building forts at the bottom of Mansfield Road.

While pounding and fixing never became my livelihood, they did serve me throughout life in recycling and creating the environments in which I lived, bringing me to The Bronx, back to New London, then on to Philadelphia, Bellows Falls and even an 1840 Fachhaus in eastern Germany.

In many respects, we aren't really the owners of where we live and work; we're the caretakers.

You can reach me by email: lostnewlondon@gmail.com
For more related Lost New London material, visit www.lostnewlondon.com